CORE INDICATORS OF EFFECTIVENESS

FOR COMMUNITY COLLEGES

THIRD EDITION

CORE INDICATORS OF EFFECTIVENESS

FOR COMMUNITY COLLEGES

THIRD EDITION

Richard Alfred
Christopher Shults
Jeffrey Seybert

Community College Press®
a division of the American Association of Community Colleges
Washington, DC

The American Association of Community Colleges (AACC) is the primary advocacy organization for the nation's community colleges. The association represents more than 1,100 two-year, associate degree–granting institutions and more than 11 million students. AACC promotes community colleges through six strategic action areas: national and international recognition and advocacy, learning and accountability, leadership development, economic and workforce development, connectedness across AACC membership, and international and intercultural education. Information about AACC and community colleges may be found at www.aacc.nche.edu.

Cover Design: Dodds Design
Interior Design: Brian Gallagher Design
Editor: Deanna D'Errico
Printer: Kirby Lithographic, Inc.

Community College Press
American Association of Community Colleges
One Dupont Circle, NW
Suite 410
Washington, DC 20036

Printed in the United States of America

Library of Congress Cataloging-in-Publication Data

Alfred, Richard L.
　　Core indicators of effectiveness for community colleges / Richard Alfred, Christopher Shults, Jeffrey Seybert.—3rd ed.
　　　　p. cm.
Previous ed. entered under title.
Includes bibliographical references.
　　"Describes 16 core indicators that community colleges can use to develop an assessment tool using quantitative data for measuring their effectiveness"—Provided by publisher.
　　　　ISBN 13: 978-0-87117-381-2
　　　　1. Community colleges—Evaluation. 2. Educational evaluation. 3. Educational indicators.
I. Shults, Christopher. II. Seybert, Jeffrey A. III. Title.

LB2328.C6912 2007
378.1'543—dc　　　　　　　　　　　　　　　　　　　　　　222007013375

CONTENTS

PREFACE

The rapid evolution of e-business, the emergence of new forms of competition, the movement toward a global economy, the tragic events of September 11, and the war on terrorism have occurred or are under way since the second edition of *Core Indicators of Effectiveness for Community Colleges* was published. These events have forced most organizations to reexamine their priorities and to place more emphasis on providing value to stakeholders in an environment in which change is the only constant. The shifting of boundaries between people and organizations is the defining characteristic of this environment.

The once-clear lines defining individual roles in colleges and universities have become blurred. Technology has made it easier to acquire and use information and to pursue learning opportunities in new ways, unconstrained by time and space. Instructors trying to remain abreast of advanced knowledge face challenges similar to those faced by students trying to master new skills and competencies. The learning environment is changing, shifting emphasis from teaching to learning and from local to global. Distinctions between teacher and learner, secondary and postsecondary learning, local and global markets, and the boundaries of heretofore discrete entities are in flux. When added to demographic and economic transformations, intensifying competition, and shifts in the distribution of wealth and power among nations, it is easy to see that the context for effectiveness is changing.

We wrote this edition of *Core Indicators* in the last quarter of 2006. Anyone reading a newspaper or magazine, watching the evening news, or surfing the Internet was likely to find headlines focused on

- global warming
- war or the threat of war on multiple fronts
- terrorism and homeland security

- declining market share for domestic automakers
- the emergence of new economic superpowers—China and India
- the preparedness of school-age U.S. youth in a world of hypercompetition
- declining stature of the United States in world opinion
- petroleum dependence and increased energy consumption
- global competition
- advances in health and biotechnology
- increasing health-care and infrastructure costs

These challenges are global in scope but local in impact through their influence on the goods and services we acquire, the prices we pay, and the life and work issues that we face each day. Thinking globally and acting locally has never been more necessary for organizations. It is a mantra that community colleges will need to embrace as they attempt to measure and improve their effectiveness in a world of new players, new rules, and ever-more demanding learners—a world of disequilibrium and hypercompetition.

Increasingly, for-profit and nonprofit organizations, including community colleges, are finding that to thrive they must compete with organizations around the world. The emergence of world-class companies in developing nations poses a major challenge to the supremacy of established economies like those of the United States, Japan, and Western Europe. Rather than contending with competition among three or four countries that have long dominated global commerce, we now face fierce challenges from multinational firms in China, India, Brazil, Mexico, and Russia. These firms are shaking up entire industries from farm equipment and appliances to aircraft and telecom services; they will become influential players in a global higher education industry. Their key advantages are access to some of the world's most dynamic growth markets and immense pools of low-cost resources, be they production workers, engineers, land, or petroleum.

But these firms are about much more than low cost. The best multinationals are proving to be as innovative and as expertly run as any in business, astutely anticipating global consumer trends and moving new products and services faster to market than are their rivals. They can tap the same or better talent, information, and capital as can Western companies, and rapidly developing school systems will supply these firms with expertly trained workers over the long term.

The implications of this challenge for community colleges will involve a shift from a local to a global focus in the measurement and use of information about their effectiveness. Leaders, faculty, and staff need to recognize that the contributions of their institutions are no longer limited to a community or to a region but extend to the nation as well. Colleges will need to broaden the horizon for measuring their effectiveness to include the impact of local efforts on a regional and national scale.

The model we present in this edition differs from that presented in the last edition in several ways. To emphasize the importance of thinking globally about effectiveness, we have added a new mission, "contribution to the public good." We have folded the "developmental skills" mission into the "general education" mission in the belief that threshold capabilities in reading, writing, and mathematics produced through developmental courses are a vital part of the general education mission of community colleges. We have also broadened the scope of the model to include the regional and national impact of stakeholders.

A growing number of colleges have invested in assessment by hiring staff and acquiring state-of-the-art technology to gather, analyze, and report information. Unfortunately, many colleges lack the resources to organize and carry out a comprehensive assessment program. Recognizing that capacity differences among colleges are real, in this edition we present a stage model for assessment (see chapter 2). Using this model, colleges may tailor their approaches to assessment to their resources, their internal capability for assessment, and the degree of difficulty associated with measurement.

The key to success in today's competitive environment is meeting the needs of key stakeholders who may have competing interests. Community colleges must meet the challenge to deliver value and to measure performance in ways that are meaningful to different groups. Forward-looking institutions are investing in assessment and capitalizing on its returns. Unfortunately, many colleges do not have the resources, the technology, or the capability to engage in a comprehensive institutional effectiveness and student outcomes assessment program. Too many institutions leave themselves vulnerable to policymakers' questions about performance on traditional measures of students' success because of their continuing inability to produce credible data documenting student and institutional performance. And, ultimately, all community colleges are going to face questions about their contribution to something beyond their own stakeholders and immediate community: the well-being of the nation.

We hope that this edition of *Core Indicators of Effectiveness* will be as useful as the first and second editions in helping practitioners tackle important issues in assessment of effectiveness. Beyond this, we hope that it will shed light on emerging challenges, while helping colleges to answer pressing questions from new and continuing stakeholders in a dynamically changing postsecondary education environment.

Richard Alfred

CHAPTER 1

The Changing Context For Effectiveness

As community colleges expand their horizons from local to global, transformational forces are compelling them to raise critical questions, to make hard choices, and to implement necessary changes so that they can improve performance. Institutions are responding by involving stakeholders more deliberately in decisions about programs and resources. Aggressive alliances between colleges and their constituencies are replacing arm's-length transactions, and intangibles such as service, innovation, and flexibility have become essential to success. New indicators of performance are drawing interest and becoming part of the effectiveness equation. Among the transformational forces at work inside and outside colleges, five are so pervasive that to ignore them is to invite trouble: changing markets, globalization, advanced technology, performance and accountability, and the emergence of networks.

Changing Markets

STUDENTS WITH CHANGING NEEDS AND EXPECTATIONS

A wave of students with incremental needs and expectations is hitting community college campuses. Students and stakeholders outside college walls, such as employers and policymakers, are becoming progressively more critical of the quality of the service that colleges render. They expect institutions and staff to seek their opinions, to listen to what they have to say, and to act on information in ways that meet or exceed their expectations. The message that students are conveying to institutions is clear and compelling: "I want terrific service. I want convenience. I want quality. Classes need to be available 24 hours a day, and parking needs to be close to the building in which I am taking classes." Students do not want to pay for anything they are not using (see Levine & Cureton, 1998). They want convenience, responsiveness, and flexibility, and they want it now or they will go somewhere else to find it.

Three distinct attributes of this intensifying demand have important implications for effectiveness. A college's program to measure effectiveness must include assessment of not only (1) its ability to meet current needs, but also (2) its ability to deliver what stakeholders expect in a way that (3) matches or exceeds the efforts of competitors. Students have a constantly expanding array of postsecondary education options and quickly become familiar with programs and services they once considered novel. The more experience they have with a program or service, the more discerning they become about their own needs and the variety of ways available for meeting those needs (see Alfred, 2000). As they gain more experience with and exposure to what institutions have to offer and become familiar with other options, their needs begin to shift and their expectations rise. Raised expectations are difficult to diminish. They elevate the standards against which students express satisfaction and create a new level of service expectation.

New Competitors

Until recently, competition involved predictable relationships among known competitors in a stable market. Today, of course, the environment is one of rapid and turbulent change. New competitors are reshaping the postsecondary education market. The University of Phoenix, one of the fastest-growing education institutions in the world, serves 200,000 students on 190 campuses and an online campus with complete degree programs. Phoenix is not alone. A growing number of for-profit higher education companies (e.g., DeVry, Inc.; ITT Educational Services; Education Management Corporation; and Corinthian College, Inc.) have set up shop in modern facilities near community college campuses.

Other players include electronic and Internet industry giants, corporate universities, course software developers, and networks created out of public–private partnerships. Virtual providers and electronic campuses (including community colleges) proliferate, all without geographical boundaries (see McClenney, 1998). Finally, changing boundaries between public and private institutions, degree and nondegree programs, and secondary and postsecondary education encourage the development of new program structures and delivery options. For example, the senior year of high school is being disaggregated and gradually being replaced by education options provided through a host of organizations—community colleges, business and industry, electronic providers, community service organizations, and more—all tied directly to students' interests (see Alfred, 2005).

In a competitive market, success comes to organizations that distinguish themselves in the eyes of customers (see Alfred, 2005). The University of Phoenix, for example, stands out because it has developed systems to quickly design and deliver programs customized to the needs of adult learners. Electronic and cable companies make education convenient through distance delivery into homes, community centers, shopping malls, and just about anywhere people congregate. Corporate training programs provide unique ways of connecting education and work. For example, Cisco Systems, Inc., and Motorola have developed customized training programs that provide workers with transportable skill sets. And we should not overlook the reputation for customer service that some proprietary institutions have established by reinventing processes such as student intake, placement, and financial aid.

Globalization

Community colleges are now operating in a postsecondary knowledge industry that defies the traditional boundaries of place and time that structured relationships among institutions in the past. Colleges that want to grow and thrive will have no choice but to embrace the forces of globalization and change now affecting the postsecondary education market. Foreign-based firms employ an increasing share of U.S. workers in domestic manufacturing and nonmanufacturing jobs. The outsourcing of white-collar and blue-collar jobs to nations with lower-cost skilled labor, such as India, China, and Korea, continues unabated. Education providers throughout the world are offering services to learners of all ages and backgrounds. For example,

- A professional in India offers tutoring in math via the Internet to a suburban Chicago high school student.
- A for-profit hospital in Cambodia offers distance-delivery courses in biotechnology to adult learners in developed nations.
- A leading-edge corporate strategist in Europe offers a seminar for credit to college and university students in the United States.

A new definition of the postsecondary education industry is developing. Twenty-five years ago the market was controlled by traditional colleges and universities offering synchronous courses and services to a narrowly defined population. Now many different providers offer courses and services to students from any place at any time. Sentiment in the United States is shifting to align with realities of the global market. Today, products and services created by foreign companies are marketed and sold in high volume in this country, domestic and foreign companies routinely merge to create advantage in world markets, foreign companies maintain regional headquarters here, and a growing number of skilled professionals trained in other countries are working in U.S. companies. The ubiquitous presence of imported products, services, and workers makes globalism a much less sensitive issue for the United States than it was at the beginning of the millennium. It also poses a challenge to colleges and universities: They need to incorporate global thinking into their business models if they are not to be left behind.

The response of most community colleges to the global imperative has been incremental, increasing foreign language offerings and arranging cultural exchanges and study-abroad opportunities. Some enterprising colleges have revamped the curriculum to incorporate culturally diverse learning styles, cross-cultural learning, and intergroup dialogue to combat ethnocentrism. Although these are useful tactics to prepare learners for work and life in a global world, they center on aspects of globalism traditionally expected from colleges and universities. To fully respond to the global imperative, community colleges will need to consider the local impact of events occurring on a global stage. What will be the impact on regional workers of the entry of China into the World Trade Organization, or the impact of global warming on availability of goods and services in local economies, or the impact of industrialization in developing countries on energy demand and pricing?

Advanced Technology

External forces are driving heightened expectations for technology on community college campuses. One factor is the increase in computer ownership: Well more than half of U.S. homes have at least one computer. In 1997, for the first time, computers outsold televisions. Internet use in the United States and Canada is growing at a pace that exceeds all projections. Today, the majority of U.S. public schools have Internet access.

In the United States, corporate spending on information technology annually exceeds expenditures for manufacturing technology. Computer technology is everywhere, cutting across income categories and education and occupation lines. Technicians, farmers, small business owners, office workers, and degreed professionals all use computers in their daily work.

Demography also fosters expectations about the impact of technology on community colleges. Demographic data point to a constantly rising demand for access to postsecondary education but a corresponding decline in campus capacity. The large-scale movement toward distance education has fueled an expectation among state officials that technology can resolve pressing capacity problems for less money than the costs associated with expanding campus facilities, building new campuses, or hiring more faculty. Policymakers weighing different options for capacity-building have found distance delivery to be a convenient answer to the demand versus capacity problem.

In a best-case scenario, distance delivery is a preferred alternative for learners and institutions seeking access to education programs and services. In a worst-case scenario, it is a convenient alternative to traditional place-based, credit-for-contact education models that are too expensive to meet the rising demand for education services. Irrespective of the view taken, technology has a profound effect on every aspect of education: what students learn, how they learn, and where they learn. Its impact is likely to spread to even broader domains affecting not only how colleges and universities deliver services to students, but with whom they partner in delivery and how benefits and value received are measured.

Performance and Accountability

Pressure on colleges to document their performance in light of accountability standards has been mounting since the 1970s, and it increased significantly in the 1990s with the passage of the Student Right-to-Know and Campus Security Act of 1990 (now integrated into Title IV of the Higher Education Act, last amended in 1998). As a result of the incorporation of this act into HEA, institutions have been federally mandated to compile and release graduation rates to students and report them to the U.S. Department of Education. Congressional probes into college costs in the late 1990s further intensified focus on accountability measures. More recently, in 2006, a federal commission created by Secretary of Education Margaret Spellings to examine issues of access, affordability, accountability, quality, and innovation in higher education concluded that higher education is too often a system based on reputation rather than on performance and recommended that states measure learning through standardized testing for all college students. Elected officials, government agencies, and business and industry employers also embrace the call for greater focus on accountability, expressing concern that the United States is falling behind other countries at a time when education is more important to our economic prosperity than ever.

This concern is more than the current **cause célèbre** or a passing fancy. A 2006 report issued by the National Center for Public Policy and Higher Education warns that poor U.S. educational performance is endangering the nation's future economic competitiveness. The nation ranks seventh worldwide in the proportion of citizens aged 25 to 34 with a college degree. On a list of 27 countries, including the world's most affluent, the United States ranks 16th in the proportion of students who complete degree and certificate programs (National Center for Public Policy and Higher Education, 2006). Policymakers are deeply concerned about issues of productivity, quality, and cost in colleges and universities, and they want something to be done about it.

They are also concerned about responsible stewardship of public funds. This issue is beginning to manifest itself as a crossover effect for higher education of the Sarbanes-Oxley Act of 2002 to curb abusive spending and illegal accounting practices in for-profit organizations. Colleges and universities will be expected to perform, to document their performance, and to be responsible for producing a return on investment. They are going to see this dynamic reflected in multiple dimensions of merit: performance indicators, performance funding, performance contracting, and performance pay.

Accountability works as both an incentive and an obstacle for colleges. As an incentive, it pushes colleges to develop performance models and measures at a faster pace than would result from natural organizational processes. As an obstacle, it can limit the interpretation of institutional performance to subjective criteria based on limited experience. All too often, criteria driving accountability expectations may have little or nothing to do with the mission of the institution or its performance (see chapter 4).

Two decades of rhetoric and effort have led to many gains in performance assessment. A growing number of colleges can produce credible data documenting students' academic performance and progress. In part this is due to changing accreditation guidelines, but it is also a result of investment in assessment and enhancement of institutional capacity. Many colleges continue to be vulnerable, however, to policymakers' questions about performance on traditional measures of students' success (i.e., graduation rates, time to degree, retention, and transfer rates). And they continue to experience difficulty in persuading policymakers to pursue alternative measures of performance because data are not adequately organized and presented to make the case.

Emergence of Networks

Driven by radical, fast-moving changes in their internal and external environments, community colleges and organizations like them are evolving into a new organizational form, best described as a network. The network, premised on a pattern of synergy and collaboration among multiple organizations, differs fundamentally from the hierarchical structures that have dominated in the past. Intensifying environmental forces, particularly those emanating from globalization of competition, resource reduction, and advanced technology, are beginning to drive changes in how colleges organize, support and manage growth, and deliver services to students and stakeholders. Most obvious are differences in the extent of decentralization of authority and responsibility for decision making and increasing reliance on external organizations to support growth and carry out operations. Reliance on external organizations to get things done lies at the heart of the network. Examples include outsourcing services to for-profit vendors, delivering distance education through consortia, sharing technology with K–12 schools, sharing facilities and equipment with business and industry, and financing and operating buildings in partnership with external organizations.

The emergence of networks will enlarge the scope of institutional effectiveness assessment by broadening the array of performance indicators requiring measurement to satisfy a new mix of players in the network. For example, a community college working in collaboration with business and industry employers, K–12 schools, and agencies of local government to increase the number of students graduating from high school and moving on to college will need to include indicators of student performance prior to college in its assessment portfolio. Likewise, a college partnering with a hospital to design and deliver a new health technology program will need to include not only "user satisfaction" in its assessment portfolio, but also "value added" and "return on investment." The inclusion of new players, however, does not automatically translate into new indicators of performance. What it does mean is that network performance is as important as institutional performance, and colleges will need to focus on both in assessing their effectiveness.

Implications for Effectiveness

Most colleges tend to focus their assessment portfolio on elements of performance internal to the institution (e.g., mission achievement and student performance and progress). However, as colleges rely more on engagement with and support from external stakeholders, they will need to supplement traditional academic indicators of performance with other indicators. Lacking suitable evidence of performance, stakeholders will not readily commit resources to higher education institutions that do not meet their expectations, or that appear not to (see Alfred, 2000). Employers will not enter into contractual relationships with colleges that do not meet their quality, cost, and service requirements. Four-year colleges and universities will be reluctant to admit students from community colleges that fail to provide students with an adequate foundation in basic skills. Accrediting agencies will sanction colleges that do not compile and report information on education outcomes. Agencies of state and local government will be reluctant to commit resources to institutions that cannot produce evidence of engagement in economic development activities.

To meet this challenge, community colleges will need to ensure that the models and measures they use in assessing effectiveness are flexible and dynamic and can change to fit the demands of the market. High-performing institutions will move beyond conventional approaches and will continually reexamine their approach to effectiveness assessment in the context of current and emerging market forces. They will document performance using indicators that reflect the needs and expectations of multiple stakeholders.

CHAPTER 2

Assessing Effectiveness

What Is Effectiveness?

Effectiveness is a construct involving multiple constituencies that hold specific (and sometimes conflicting) expectations about what a college should be doing and the results it should produce. For this reason, it is difficult to define and even more difficult to measure. Adding to this difficulty are changes in the conceptualization of effectiveness caused by variation in contextual conditions. For example, the shift from a local to a global stage, an ever-shifting array of stakeholders, and the constantly changing environment in which colleges operate encourage change in both the conceptualization and definition of effectiveness. Like organizations in health-care and the corporate sectors, community colleges are being challenged by competitors in a market without boundaries or rules of engagement and from rapidly changing fiscal and political conditions. This challenge leads to two conditions: (1) resource constraints associated with changing federal and state spending priorities and (2) new calls for accountability that have resulted in demands for increased productivity.

Despite these conditions, the heart of any definition of institutional effectiveness remains the ability of an institution to match its performance to the purposes established in its mission and vision statements (see Ewell, 1992) and to the needs and expectations of its stakeholders (see Alfred, 2005). This implies that the outcomes generated by an institution are the ultimate measure of effectiveness (see definition of outcomes on page 11). It also implies that an effective institution can conclusively document the outcomes it produces in support of its mission and can do so for different stakeholders. However, two important caveats surround this definition.

First, both the mission of the institution and the outcomes it generates must be consistent with a growing variety of stakeholders' needs. No college, regardless of the quality of its graduates, can be considered effective if its results are incongruent with clients' needs and expectations. As a consequence, specific judgments of institutional effectiveness will not be uniform. Instead, they will vary according to the needs and expectations of different stakeholders (see Alfred & Kreider, 1991). An institution's willingness and capacity to determine and quickly respond to stakeholders' needs is, therefore, an integral part of effectiveness.

Second, colleges must produce results efficiently, that is, within the constraints of available resources. Under current financial and public policy conditions, only a small number of community colleges will be able to meet stakeholders' needs without incurring increased costs. Efficiency and effectiveness are entirely different concepts, and college leaders would be well advised to ensure that simple efficiency measures are not substituted for important indicators of effectiveness (see Alfred, 1998). The wise use and responsible stewardship of resources in the pursuit of mission-related goals is an integral part of the effectiveness equation for any college. In the absence of performance measures that cover a wide range of outcomes, however, efficiency is not sufficient to determine a college's effectiveness.

Figure 2.1 depicts the key elements of effectiveness and their interrelationships. A community college is effective when its results match its mission, but both

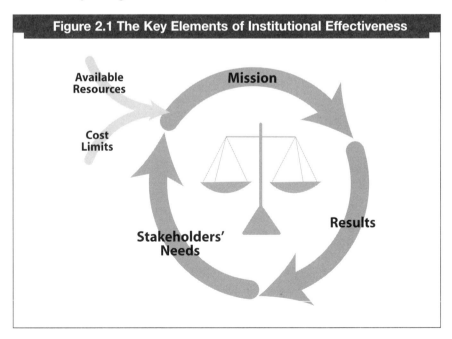

Figure 2.1 The Key Elements of Institutional Effectiveness

mission and results must also match (or exceed) stakeholders' needs and expectations. These relationships must be maintained within the limits of costs and available resources irrespective of institutional context and circumstances.

Defining and Measuring Core Indicators

Leaders and staff who are interested and engaged in institutional effectiveness assessment face many challenges when designing a system. One of them is to identify the boundaries of the system, that is, what to assess and why. It is always tempting to add more indicators to ensure that everything that could possibly be important to assess is included. Assessment systems loaded with too many indicators, however, change the focus from using information to improve performance to managing a system to acquire information. Means and ends become inverted and the entire purpose of assessment—enhancement of performance—is lost. The objective of a core indicator is to reduce the task of effectiveness assessment to the most important indices of college performance. The following definitions and guidelines provide parameters for a discussion of core indicators.

OUTCOMES
Outcomes are the results generated by a college, while addressing the needs of important stakeholders, through education-related activities. Most often they take the form of near-term results occurring during or shortly after college: a course grade, a degree or certificate, transfer to a 4-year college, attainment of a particular skill, or acquisition of a job related to an academic program. Outcomes, however, also take the form of longer-term results, such as general education competencies leading to job promotion or involvement in civic affairs. Colleges that are effective create outcomes that are meaningful to and for multiple stakeholders.

INDICATORS
An *indicator* is a regularly produced measure that describes a specified condition or result that a college can gather information on, examine and report on, and use regularly and systematically as a tool for planning, assessment, and decision making. Indicators relate to virtually everything that a college does and, for this reason, can be reported in terms of a wide range of performance outcomes (e.g., student satisfaction with courses and services, facilities utilization, employer perceptions of program quality, economic impact, cost efficiency, staff perceptions of college climate, etc.).

CORE INDICATORS

A *core indicator* is a regularly produced measure that describes a specified condition or result that is central (or foundational) to the achievement of a college's mission and to meeting the needs and interests of key stakeholders. The difference between an indicator and a core indicator is not always easy to discern. We offer the following example to draw a contrast between the concepts. Student progress lies at the heart of any college's statement of mission and purpose, whereas a measure of operational efficiency such as facilities utilization would generally not be viewed as central to mission achievement. Consequently, a college would be likely to assign high value to indicators of student progress such as retention, goal achievement, or degree completion to determine the extent to which it is achieving its mission. It would not assign a similar value to facilities utilization.

MEASUREMENT GUIDELINES

The measurement of core indicators should reflect and support sound assessment practice. Practitioners can use the following checklist of questions to ensure that assessment efforts conform to accepted practice and that specific measures will be useful in determining effectiveness.

❑ Is the indicator supported by a comprehensive information system?
❑ Is the indicator part of a commitment to track important data over time, thereby ensuring that effectiveness assessment is a continuous improvement process?
❑ Is there a standard of comparison or a benchmark against which progress can be measured?
❑ Is the reliability of the indicator regularly assessed? Are changes made when needed?
❑ Is the indicator credible to college personnel who are in a position to change institutional behavior?
❑ Can the indicator be readily understood by external decision makers? Is it salient and credible to them?
❑ Does the indicator provide information that will help the institution to improve? Does it encourage the institution to value the right things and to take action?
❑ Does the indicator reflect the perspectives and concerns of multiple constituencies?
❑ Can data be obtained for the indicator at reasonable cost?

Modeling the Core Indicators

A model is an abstraction of reality used to improve understanding of complex concepts such as effectiveness. If effectiveness is defined as the capacity of a college to match its results with its mission, vision, and goals, as well as with the needs of its stakeholders, all within the limits of costs and available resources, what would an effectiveness model look like? We know that community colleges have many stakeholders, but are they equally important? We also know that stakeholders view colleges differently depending on what is important to them; they have different performance expectations associated with different needs. Finally, we know that colleges cannot measure everything. Efficiency is important: The focus must be restricted to a small number of indicators reflecting the needs and interests of key constituencies.

These observations constitute the foundation of a comprehensive model of effectiveness, which is illustrated in Figure 2.2 on page 21. Key elements of this model are the stakeholders internal and external to the college, the missions commonly pursued by community colleges, and the core indicators representative of outcomes generated in specific missions. The following example illustrates how the model works: The graduation rates indicator is included in the student progress mission. Because this indicator is important to a number of stakeholders both internal and external to a college, it is core to the assessment of effectiveness. The same is true of all 16 indicators defined as core.

The core indicators are not random, isolated measures. As the model shows, they connect the mission of a college and the results it produces with the needs of its stakeholders. Practitioners are encouraged to use the model as a basis for reviewing existing assessment systems or as a tool for developing new systems.

Relationship of Core Indicators to Mission

In this section, we describe the key themes of 6 missions and explain how 16 core indicators can be used to measure outcomes related to those missions. (See Table 3.1 on page 23 for an outline of all of the missions and indicators.)

STUDENT PROGRESS

Student progress can be measured in terms of actual achievement as well as students' perceptions of an institution's contribution to their achievement. The progress and satisfaction measures suggested by the core indicators supporting the student's progress mission gauge the effectiveness of colleges in relation to their open-door mission by providing an overall picture of students' success. Measuring both progress and satisfaction reinforces the understanding that achievement and satisfaction are integrally related and that measuring them requires tracking the intentions, behavior, and perceptions of students over time.

The *student goal attainment* indicator seeks to capture individual intent and then trace its achievement. It is the most important of the student progress indicators because it is a determinant of the aspiration that drives learners forward in the pursuit of goals. *Student satisfaction,* a measure of the relationship between what students want or expect from college and what they receive, is included because it is also a pervasive factor in students' success. In a market replete with competitors and education options, students often base a decision to stay at or leave a college on feelings of satisfaction or dissatisfaction. The other two indicators, *persistence* and *graduation rates,* follow the behavior of entering cohorts of students and are less descriptive. We include them here not only because state and federal government agencies frequently mandate tracking data for them, but also because they can become useful tools when incorporated into a larger effort to chart student progress. The danger lies in misinterpreting these aggregate data by applying traditional academic assumptions about students' aspirations, persistence, and degree completion to the much broader range of intent and behavior that community college students exhibit in contrast to their 4-year college counterparts.

GENERAL EDUCATION

An important goal of education is to strengthen both general skills and broad analytical capabilities that students need to function competently in life. The general education mission has grown in importance and complexity in recent years. Students today must not only possess skills such as writing and problem solving, but also apply these skills in an increasingly interdependent, culturally diverse world. College-educated adults must now have a global understanding of the world in which they live and work, they must appreciate and understand diversity, and they must be comfortable with change.

To assess effectiveness in meeting the general education mission, we recommend three broad core indicators: *success in subsequent and related course work, program learning outcomes and mastery of discipline,* and *demonstration of general education competencies* (e.g., communication, critical thinking, problem solving, and interpersonal skills). At a minimum, information gathered for these indicators should extend beyond the accumulation of credits. Assessment should include feedback from groups and organizations outside of the college that are affected by the skills and competencies acquired by students.

Because learning includes both basic and higher-order abilities, is developed across the curriculum, and is best demonstrated through the application of knowledge, measuring achievement requires sophisticated forms of assessment. Practitioners have tried many strategies with varying degrees of success. Community colleges will need to continue to test and refine existing methodologies and develop their own for measuring learning.

OUTREACH
The outreach mission of community colleges grows out of, and feeds into, the economic, social, and cultural circumstances of a regional or local setting. The relationship between college and community is dynamic and unique. It requires that colleges (a) remain alert to local and regional needs, as well as needs beyond the region that are part of the larger world, and (b) respond on a timely basis with programs and services that meet identified or anticipated needs.

We recommend two indicators to determine effectiveness in the outreach mission: *regional market penetration rates* and *responsiveness to community needs. Penetration rates* refers to the proportion of citizens in a defined service region involved in some way with a college (enrollment in credit and noncredit courses, committee membership, attendance at meetings or events, etc.). A statistical measure of this type can be particularly useful in helping decision makers gauge the extent of connectivity between a college and its community and, with additional demographic data collection, whether there is appropriate, proportional representation from various segments of the community in college programs and services. Because community development includes identifying and reaching out to underserved populations, this indicator becomes a valuable mechanism for identifying gaps in service.

Measuring effectiveness for the outreach mission is not easy. Unlike other aspects of mission that are defined in less situational terms, a college's linkage with its community grows out of specific needs and opportunities, and evaluation is idiosyncratic. For this reason, we suggest no one methodology for measuring these core indicators beyond the general rule that colleges must in some way identify a client, determine the client's needs, and measure the client's satisfaction with the college's response. In addition, practitioners must monitor indicators over time if they are to become true indexes of penetration and responsiveness.

WORKFORCE DEVELOPMENT

Global competition, advanced technology, and the outsourcing and offshoring of jobs have created dynamically changing conditions in the job market that require constant vigilance if career and technical programs are to keep pace with the changing needs of employers. Community colleges must monitor market conditions closely and regularly assess employer needs for workforce development as well as their satisfaction with community college graduates. More workers are turning to quick-response noncredit programs for career education because they now understand that it is as important to continue to upgrade skills as it is to initially acquire them. Workforce readiness has become an ongoing task that requires a variety of programmatic responses.

Core indicators need to reflect these dynamics and routinely include assessment of career preparation. The following guidelines will help in this process. First, do not base the evaluation of students' career goals solely on certificate or degree completion. Collect data specific to objective indicators such as *licensure and certification pass rates* and *placement rates,* as well as *client satisfaction with programs and services* (clients include all those coming into contact with a college, including employers). Employers' feedback should also be sought on the adequacy of workers' knowledge and skills and their potential for career growth. Finally, attempt to measure outcomes of noncredit courses and services, as well as credit programs in workforce development.

CONTRIBUTION TO THE PUBLIC GOOD

Community colleges contribute in important ways to the betterment of people and communities—the public good—by creating value through access to better jobs, enhancement of earning potential, improvement in the quality of life, attraction and retention of business and industry, and much more. Although the addition of value through engagement with the public has always been a focus of assessment, it is of particular interest to elected officials seeking to better their communities and policymakers seeking assurances that workers will possess knowledge and skills that enable U.S. businesses to compete on a global scale.

We propose a single core indicator, *value added to the community,* to assess effectiveness with this mission. It presents a useful way for colleges to determine how well they are performing as they deliver education services to constituencies on a much larger scale than that of individuals and organizations. To assess value added, colleges will need to first identify the scope and boundaries of the community being served, determine the different dimensions of value for the community, and measure the extent to which value has been added through services delivered. Measuring value is a complex task rendered difficult by the fact that communities have different notions of value: how it is defined, how it is experienced and realized, and the difference it must make to be recognized as value.

TRANSFER PREPARATION

Transfer preparation is an important mission for internal and external stakeholders of community colleges, and it is particularly appealing to policymakers. This is because it is a cost-effective strategy that broadens the impact of public education by making the first 2 years of college more accessible. Unfortunately, many policymakers continue to assume that many, perhaps most, community college students will move readily through course work, transfer to a 4-year college or university, and attain a bachelor's degree. Because this is often not the case, assessment of transfer preparation must track individual students to document transfer patterns. Practitioners commonly use two indicators to track transfer students: *transfer rates* and *performance after transfer.* Although recording students' intent to transfer is a logical and essential first step in this process, early statements of intent made by students are frequently unreliable. Thus, to avoid mistakes in subsequent measurement, colleges should monitor and update the number and rate of actual transfers each semester or year.

This course of action suggests the following ground rules: First, obtain information from students about their transfer intentions at reasonable intervals beyond their entry into college. Then, obtain information about their behaviors as evidence of whether they achieved what they intended (i.e., did they transfer as intended?). Continuous assessment should provide answers to the following questions: Has the student enrolled for more than one semester, earned a designated number of credits, or filed a degree plan? Exercise caution in measuring transfer success. Avoid equating success with certificate- and degree-completion rates at the community college, because many students move between colleges, programs, and courses for personal reasons.

Core indicators in this category provide insights into effectiveness at two different levels of analysis. The transfer rates indicator is suited to a systemwide rather than institutional level of analysis, because transfer goals may vary from community to community and from college to college. Data descriptive of performance after transfer can be usefully compared from college to college.

Assessment Using a Stage Model

Contextual variation among institutions (size and complexity, finances, service region trends, the needs and interests of specific constituencies, mix of programs and services, etc.) will render some indicators more or less important depending on an institution's circumstances. Furthermore, colleges have different capacities for assessment. Although a growing number of institutions have invested in technology and expert staff to gather, analyze, and report information, some colleges lack the time, money, or staff to conduct a full assessment program. The result is a reduced capacity for assessing effectiveness and a need to pare back to essentials.

Given these realities, we have developed a stage model for assessing effectiveness, to accommodate the differing capacities of colleges. The model, depicted in Figure 2.3 (see page 22), shows the core indicators in boldface. Additional indicators worthy of consideration in assessment appear in standard print. Capacity is depicted as a composite of three factors that interact to determine what an institution is capable of doing in assessment:

- *difficulty*—extent and degree of rigor associated with measuring specific indicators
- *resources*—funds, staff, and technology available for assessment
- *capability*—expertise among staff to carry out assessment

The essential indicators for assessing effectiveness—the absolute minimum for all institutions—are depicted in the category labeled "compulsory indicators." These are indicators that must be measured in all institutions, regardless of capacity, because of situational realities and external mandates (accreditation, federal and state reporting requirements, governing board bylaws, etc.). The difficulty associated with assessment in the compulsory category is low for some indicators and high for others, but assessment must be ongoing because these indicators are high on the radar screens of important stakeholders. Institutions with limited capacities for assessment will want to consider using these indicators as the foundation for their assessment program and making careful choices about what to measure beyond them.

A second category of indicators involving a higher degree of difficulty and requiring more capability is "indicators of engagement." These indicators focus on measuring stakeholders' involvement, satisfaction, and benefits received through affiliation with a college. They are important for all institutions, but pose a challenge for institutions with limited resources and capability for assessment. Core indicators that rise to the top in this category are student goal attainment, student satisfaction, responsiveness to community needs, regional market penetration rates, and employer satisfaction with graduates. Because engagement can take many forms, measuring its achievement requires sophisticated forms of assessment. Colleges with resources and expertise may have the capacity to develop and test new methodologies or refine existing methodologies. Those lacking resources will need to make careful choices about which indicators to measure in this category.

Finally, recognizing that the contribution of community colleges is not limited to the local communities they serve, a category labeled "indicators of macro impact"—impact on a larger scale (e.g., regional, statewide, national)—is proposed. Indicators in this category, such as economic impact and contribution to community well-being, are difficult to measure and require a significant investment. Only those institutions with the most advanced technology and the highest resources will have the capacity to work comfortably with indicators in this category. Macro (or global) impact through local effort is, however, something that all colleges will need to factor into their thinking about effectiveness. Ultimately, colleges must be able to assess their impact on a scale that extends not only to their communities but also to the region and nation.

Although all the indicators in the compulsory category are included in the portfolio of core indicators and in the technical description in chapter 3, only some of the indicators in the engagement and macro categories are designated as core indicators. Engagement indicators such as student goal attainment and employer satisfaction with graduates are designated as core indicators because they are important as a measure of an institution's success in meeting the needs of key stakeholders, and they are discrete and lend themselves to easy measurement in contrast to indicators that are more complex. Only one indicator in the macro impact category, value added to the community, is designated as a core indicator. This is because it is essential to measuring the impact of an institution on large-scale entities such as a community, a region, or a state, and ultimately, the nation, as part of the industry of higher education.

>-I-+)-+-O-+(+-I-<

Community college practitioners may not view all 16 core indicators as the best or most appropriate choices for them. An effectiveness indicator that is essential for one college may not be important for another. Therefore, practitioners should consider and adopt any additional indicators they deem to be appropriate to the circumstances of their colleges.

Furthermore, not all colleges will view the stage model we have presented as being appropriate for them. Some community colleges may view the idea that assessment capability varies among colleges as capricious and arbitrary. However, differences in capacity are a distinct reality for community colleges working with varying resources.

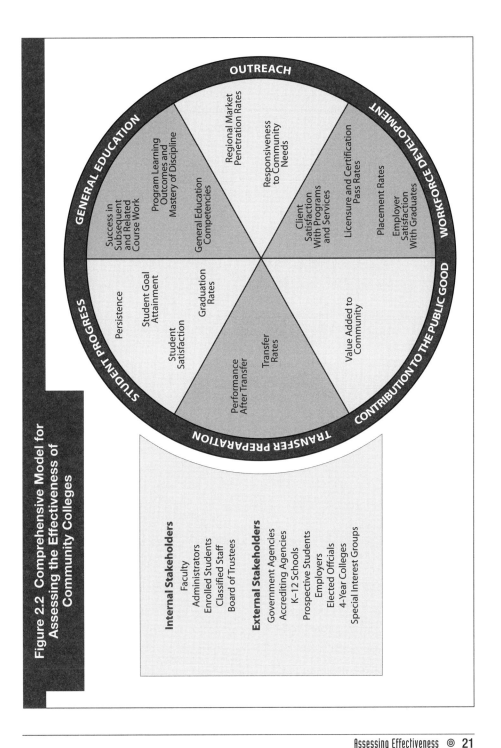

Figure 2.2 Comprehensive Model for Assessing the Effectiveness of Community Colleges

OUTREACH

GENERAL EDUCATION

WORKFORCE DEVELOPMENT

STUDENT PROGRESS

CONTRIBUTION TO THE PUBLIC GOOD

TRANSFER PREPARATION

Program Learning Outcomes and Mastery of Discipline

Success in Subsequent and Related Course Work

Regional Market Penetration Rates

Responsiveness to Community Needs

General Education Competencies

Client Satisfaction With Programs and Services

Licensure and Certification Pass Rates

Placement Rates

Employer Satisfaction With Graduates

Persistence

Student Goal Attainment

Graduation Rates

Student Satisfaction

Transfer Rates

Performance After Transfer

Value Added to Community

Internal Stakeholders
Faculty
Administrators
Enrolled Students
Classified Staff
Board of Trustees

External Stakeholders
Government Agencies
Accrediting Agencies
K–12 Schools
Prospective Students
Employers
Elected Offcials
4-Year Colleges
Special Interest Groups

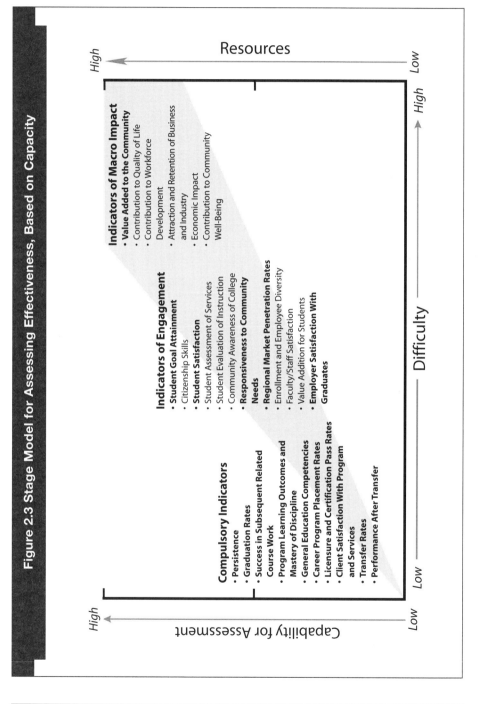

Figure 2.3 Stage Model for Assessing Effectiveness, Based on Capacity

Compulsory Indicators
- Persistence
- Graduation Rates
- Success in Subsequent Related Course Work
- Program Learning Outcomes and Mastery of Discipline
- General Education Competencies
- Career Program Placement Rates
- Licensure and Certification Pass Rates
- Client Satisfaction With Program and Services
- Transfer Rates
- Performance After Transfer

Indicators of Engagement
- Student Goal Attainment
- Citizenship Skills
- Student Satisfaction
- Student Assessment of Services
- Student Evaluation of Instruction
- Community Awareness of College
- Responsiveness to Community Needs
- Regional Market Penetration Rates
- Enrollment and Employee Diversity
- Faculty/Staff Satisfaction
- Value Addition for Students
- Employer Satisfaction With Graduates

Indicators of Macro Impact
- Value Added to the Community
- Contribution to Quality of Life
- Contribution to Workforce Development
- Attraction and Retention of Business and Industry
- Economic Impact
- Contribution to Community Well-Being

Resources — High / Low

Difficulty — Low / High

Capability for Assessment — High / Low

CHAPTER 3

Core Indicators: A Technical Description

S ome indicators of effectiveness do not readily lend themselves to measurement. To be used effectively, each needs to be carefully defined. In this chapter, we present technical descriptions for 16 core indicators, which include a working definition of what the indicators are intended to measure, recommendations on when or how often to collect data, and the recommended method of gathering data. In some instances, we also describe additional methods of gathering data and provide advice on techniques that can be used to organize and analyze data. Table 3.1 presents an outline of the 16 indicators, grouped by the mission they relate to.

Table 3.1 Core Indicators of Effectiveness for Community Colleges, by Mission

Mission: Student Progress
Core Indicator 1: Student Goal Attainment
Core Indicator 2: Persistence
Core Indicator 3: Graduation Rates
Core Indicator 4: Student Satisfaction

Mission: General Education
Core Indicator 5: Success in Subsequent and Related Course Work
Core Indicator 6: Program Learning Outcomes and Mastery of Discipline
Core Indicator 7: Demonstration of General Education Competencies

Mission: Outreach
Core Indicator 8: Regional Market Penetration Rates
Core Indicator 9: Responsiveness to Community Needs

Mission: Workforce Development
Core Indicator 10: Placement Rates
Core Indicator 11: Licensure and Certification Pass Rates
Core Indicator 12: Employer Satisfaction With Graduates
Core Indicator 13: Client Satisfaction With Programs and Services

Mission: Contribution to the Public Good
Core Indicator 14: Value Added to the Community

Mission: Transfer Preparation
Core Indicator 15: Transfer Rates
Core Indicator 16: Performance After Transfer

STUDENT PROGRESS

CORE INDICATOR 1:
STUDENT GOAL ATTAINMENT

STATISTIC OF INTEREST

The proportion of students whose goals for attaining a college education upon enrolling or during attendance in a college were met upon exit from the college.

FREQUENCY OF DATA COLLECTION

Ideally, goal-related data should be obtained twice: when a student registers and when that student exits. Additionally, data can be solicited from currently enrolled and former students.

RECOMMENDED METHOD

Survey students using a longitudinal design that, at minimum, captures students' goals at entry and upon exit, to determine whether their goals have been met or have changed.

ADDITIONAL METHODS

Include questions in new or existing surveys of entering, currently enrolled, exiting, and former students to elicit information specifically related to goal attainment. For example, for entering or currently enrolled students, ask them to rate, on a 5-point Likert scale, how important it is to achieve specific goals such as learning to communicate better in writing, work more effectively in groups, or learn skills that will enable them to advance in their jobs. The same questions can be recast in the past tense for exiting and former students. As many as 15–20 items can be efficiently administered. The responses can yield data indicating not only the importance of specific attainment goals to students, but also how much the college contributed to their attainment of those goals.

CORE INDICATOR 2: PERSISTENCE

STATISTIC OF INTEREST

The proportion of students who enrolled for the first time at the beginning of one academic year and who (1) were still enrolled for at least one credit at the beginning of the next academic year and who (2) had not yet completed a degree or certificate.

FREQUENCY OF DATA COLLECTION

Persistence data are already collected each fall semester, as specified by HEA disclosure requirements; therefore, reporting persistence rates from fall to fall has become standard practice. Also collecting data at the beginning of every term may yield better long-term results.

RECOMMENDED METHOD

Develop a database that can be updated regularly to collect longitudinal data, to track an identified entering student cohort (i.e., all students registering for their first credits at the community college in a given term) from entry to exit using data elements such as course and program enrollment and degrees and certificates awarded (see Ewell, Parker, & Jones, 1988; Palmer, 1990).

CORE INDICATOR 3: GRADUATION RATES

STATISTIC OF INTEREST

The proportion of students who enrolled in and subsequently completed a degree or certificate program.

FREQUENCY OF DATA COLLECTION

Data related to graduation rates should be collected annually for each entering cohort beginning 2 years after initial enrollment.

RECOMMENDED METHOD

Because the majority of community college students attend part time and, therefore, may take as long as 7 or 8 years to graduate, collecting data for these students requires a methodology that tracks students beyond 2 or 4 years of college attendance. Develop a database that expands on the graduation rate data gathered via HEA reporting requirements, to include the graduation rates of all students, including part-time students, who constitute the majority of community college students. Given the sensitivity of this statistic, never present it in isolation from information describing students' goals and degree plans. And report it selectively so that attendance patterns, course taking behaviors, and intentions of different student groups are apparent. We recommend that this core indicator be reported in conjunction with Core Indicator 2: Persistence.

ADDITIONAL METHODS

- Report data for full-time, first-time-in-college students versus other students in the cohort.
- Report data according to whether students completed 12 or more credits.
- Report data according to whether students reported "degree attainment" as an initial or current goal.
- Report data separately for students reported as successfully transferring to a 4-year college or obtaining program-related employment without having earned a degree or certificate from a community college.

CORE INDICATOR 4: STUDENT SATISFACTION

STATISTIC OF INTEREST

The proportion of graduates whose college experience met or exceeded the expectations they held upon initial enrollment.

FREQUENCY OF DATA COLLECTION

At minimum, collect data from students upon the time of their exit from college—when they graduate, transfer to another college, leave college to accept a job, etc.). If possible, collect data on student satisfaction levels at more frequent intervals, while they are still enrolled.

RECOMMENDED METHOD

Using a two-part design, survey students at or near the time of their exit from college. In the first part of the survey, pose open-ended questions, asking students to identify what their specific needs and expectations were at entry; whether they changed during college; and the extent to which the college met, exceeded, or fell short of meeting their needs and expectations. In the second part of the survey, to obtain information about satisfaction with specific services and experiences, use a 5-point Likert-type scale to assess attributes of college performance such as the quality of teaching, accessibility of services, availability of tutorial assistance, aspects of convenience (e.g., close parking and Internet access). Conduct surveys by mail, electronically, or in class, with the latter methodology generally yielding the highest response rate. If resources are available, conduct focus groups and in-depth interviews with students as an enhancement to surveys.

ADDITIONAL METHODS

Organize students' ratings by
- reasons for leaving (e.g., graduation, transfer, job, etc.)
- academic program or discipline
- enrollment status (full-time vs. part-time status)

COMMENTS

Practitioners have enhanced their understanding of factors underlying student progress by linking student satisfaction to a number of indexes of institutional effectiveness, including persistence and graduation rates. Student satisfaction may be viewed within either a personal or institutional context.

CORE INDICATOR 5:
SUCCESS IN SUBSEQUENT AND RELATED COURSE WORK

STATISTIC OF INTEREST

The proportion of students identified as lacking basic skills (e.g., in reading, writing, or computation), who earned a grade of C or better in nondevelopmental college courses after having completed developmental course work.

FREQUENCY OF DATA COLLECTION

Collect data at the beginning and end of each grading period.

RECOMMENDED METHOD

Track students from entry to exit using a continuously updated longitudinal database that includes elements such as basic skills proficiency levels, types of courses enrolled in, and course grades.

ADDITIONAL METHODS

- Compare persistence and degree-completion rates for (a) the cohort with those of (b) students identified as proficient in basic skills and (c) students identified as needing, but not completing, developmental course work.
- Compare rates of successful college-level course completion with a grade of C or better for all three populations.

CORE INDICATOR 6: PROGRAM LEARNING OUTCOMES AND MASTERY OF DISCIPLINE

STATISTIC OF INTEREST

The proportion of entering students enrolled in or completing programs (a) with organized, sequential courses or (b) leading to a degree or certificate, who demonstrate a mastery of skills and competencies specific to predetermined program learning outcomes.

FREQUENCY OF DATA COLLECTION

Collect data at the beginning and end of each grading period.

RECOMMENDED METHOD

Use instructors' written observations of the skills and competencies of students (a) in capstone courses or learning experiences, (b) on a course-by-course basis, and (c) in authentic performance-based settings. In programs and disciplines for which state, regional, or national standardized licensing examinations are required for career entry, use exam scores as a substantive measure of competency attainment.

GENERAL EDUCATION

CORE INDICATOR 7:
DEMONSTRATION OF GENERAL EDUCATION COMPETENCIES

STATISTIC OF INTEREST

The proportion of students who demonstrate general education competencies during and after college attendance. *Note.* No single statistic satisfies the intent of this indicator (see Comments).

FREQUENCY OF DATA COLLECTION

At minimum, collect data at course entry and exit, course by course.

RECOMMENDED METHOD

- Maintain portfolios of students' work. Maintain electronic or hard copy portfolios of work that students produce as they progress through courses and curricula. Faculty teams can periodically examine samples of work, generally using holistic scoring rubrics. Analyze aggregate results of the scoring process to determine the extent to which students demonstrate identified competencies. Instructors can use this information to make changes in curricula and pedagogy when learners have deficiencies.
- Course-embedded assessment. Instructors can embed assessment into assignments and examinations. Treat these embedded assignments and test items like the student portfolios: Have teams of instructors analyze and aggregate data for specific competencies, using the results for curricular and pedagogical improvement.
- Testing. Use nationally normed standardized instruments, locally developed tests, or both to assess students' achievement of general education competencies.
- Alumni surveys. In follow-up surveys, ask former students about the general education competencies they gained as a result of their enrollment in courses and curricula.

CORE INDICATOR 7 [cont'd]: DEMONSTRATION OF GENERAL EDUCATION COMPETENCIES

COMMENTS

Before undertaking any methodology, colleges should identify what set of general competencies students are expected to acquire as a part of their overall learning experience. These competencies almost always include the following:

- effective written and oral communication skills
- critical thinking and problem solving
- computation
- civic engagement and responsibility
- computer skills
- appreciation and understanding of diversity and multiculturalism

Curriculum guides and course syllabi for general education courses are a good source of information for identifying general education competencies.

Once a college agrees on a particular set of general education competencies, it must ensure that those competencies are (a) taught throughout the curriculum in both transfer- and career-related courses and (b) assessed at some point at or near the close of a student's education experience.

CORE INDICATOR 8: REGIONAL MARKET PENETRATION RATES

STATISTIC OF INTEREST

The proportion of the total population aged 17 and older in the college's service area that has participated in at least one organized activity (course, program, service, event, etc.) sponsored by the college.

FREQUENCY OF DATA COLLECTION

At least annually.

RECOMMENDED METHOD

Examine attendance records for classes, events, and activities sponsored by the college, and periodically administer a community-impact survey to a representative sample of residents in the service region. This survey should contain items describing various types of contact with the college (formal and informal) and overall reactions and satisfaction rates.

ADDITIONAL METHODS

Unduplicated headcount and total attendance figures can also be usefully reported for this indicator. To measure the extent to which the population has used college facilities or programs, calculate the total number of record-ed contact hours (the duration of an event times the number of persons par-ticipating in the event) for all activities—both instructional and noninstruc-tional—divided by the service region population.

CORE INDICATOR 9: RESPONSIVENESS TO COMMUNITY NEEDS

STATISTIC OF INTEREST

The proportion of community constituents whose needs are met by the college. *Note.* No single statistic currently meets the intent of this indicator (see Comments).

FREQUENCY OF DATA COLLECTION

Ongoing.

RECOMMENDED METHOD

Responding to the intent of this indicator requires a college to engage in an ongoing process of (a) identifying the needs and expectations of the community; (b) demonstrating that it is responsive to these needs and expectations by continuously improving and adapting its programs and services; (c) demonstrating that the constituency groups served are satisfied with, and have benefited from, these programs and services; and (d) demonstrating that it actively seeks ways to establish and promote partnerships with other entities and organizations for the benefit of stakeholders or the community. A community college's stakeholders will almost always consist of distinct constituencies and subgroups whose needs and expectations must be independently assessed and determined. Meeting the challenge of this indicator will therefore require the use of multiple methods for gathering information, but more importantly, it will require the use of an established, ongoing process of planning and reviews to ensure that the information is appropriately obtained, interpreted, and acted upon by the institution.

ADDITIONAL METHODS

- Conduct periodic needs assessments with citizens in the college's service region. These are typically electronic or telephone surveys using instruments designed to collect information about current education and service needs, contact, and satisfaction with the college.
- Conduct surveys or focus groups with community organizations, citizen groups, employers, and other stakeholders, to determine needs and current levels of satisfaction.
- Use environmental scanning processes designed to systematically examine the content of printed matter (newspaper stories, reports forecasting

CORE INDICATOR 9 (cont'd): RESPONSIVENESS TO COMMUNITY NEEDS

population and employment growth, job advertisements, etc.) and employment and other socioeconomic data describing regional trends that shape and determine future needs.

- Administer specially designed evaluations periodically to participants in each program or event sponsored by a college, to assess the expectations of the participants and the degree to which their expectations were met.

- Gather data on partnerships with external organizations and agencies established in a given year, together with descriptive statistics such as the number of people served through such partnerships, their geographic distribution, and their total dollar value.

- Conduct internal audits of a college's response to a selected sample of requests—for example, to initiate a new program, offer a new service, or engage in a partnership or a joint venture. Such audits should examine both the time required to respond and the organizational obstacles encountered in attempting to do so.

COMMENTS

Measuring responsiveness can be simple or complex depending on how important the concept is for a college. For some colleges it entails a simple tabulation of the frequency with which they offer programs, services, and activities in response to expressed community needs. For others measurement amounts to a more complicated tabulation involving defining and assessing various forms of community need, institutional response, and satisfaction.

CORE INDICATOR 10: PLACEMENT RATES

STATISTIC OF INTEREST

The proportion of entering community college students acquiring a marketable skill (i.e., completion of least three career or technical courses in a particular field) who obtain employment in a field directly related to that skill within one year of last attendance.

FREQUENCY OF DATA COLLECTION

Collect data at course entry and exit and at follow-up points after exit.

RECOMMENDED METHOD

The predominant method used is a follow-up questionnaire administered periodically to former students electronically, by mail, or by telephone. If available, state employment information (generally available through a state's Department of Labor or its equivalent) provides a more direct method of assessment. The obvious limitation of this methodology is the fact that many state databases do not contain the job information needed to adequately identify occupation.

ADDITIONAL METHODS

- Report data for students according to the amount of prior credit earned at the community college and by whether a degree or certificate was earned.
- Report data for students according to occupations that are both directly and indirectly related to the student's field of training.
- Report placement rates for all students enrolling for at least one career or technical course at the community college (this relaxes the "marketable skill" restriction in the core measure).

CORE INDICATOR 11:
LICENSURE AND CERTIFICATION PASS RATES

STATISTIC OF INTEREST

The proportion of students who complete or graduate from a community college career or technical program, seek licensure or certification for the first time within a given year, and actually obtain licensure or certification.

FREQUENCY OF DATA COLLECTION

At least annually.

RECOMMENDED METHOD

Rely primarily on data obtained directly from state licensing agencies. If data are not available from licensing agencies, use a follow-up survey conducted electronically or by mail with former students or those who have completed programs. Information obtained from state agencies must be compiled on a field-by-field basis by contacting the relevant licensing or certification body. In some states, lists of such bodies are available through the state higher education executive office (SHEEO) or the office responsible for professional regulation.

ADDITIONAL METHODS

Statistics about overall licensure pass rates should be broken down by field of study to make them more meaningful. Make a distinction between fields in which licensure or certification is required for employment or practice and those in which it is not. To reflect the fact that not all fields are governed by licensure and not all students seek certification (in cases in which it is voluntary), the proportion of graduates actively seeking certification should also be reported.

CORE INDICATOR 12: EMPLOYER SATISFACTION WITH GRADUATES

STATISTIC OF INTEREST

The proportion of a sample of regional employers in a given field who indicate that their employees who are community college graduates exhibit skills and job performance that are equivalent or superior to those exhibited by other employees.

FREQUENCY OF DATA COLLECTION

Information should be collected annually or biannually from employers on record as having hired community college graduates for a 5-year period after graduation.

RECOMMENDED METHOD

Periodically conduct a cross-sectional survey of a sample of area employers using an open-ended design, asking employers to list the specific programs and institutions from which they recruit or from which they obtain their best-performing employees. Because this method yields higher response rates, it is preferred to the more typical two-phase follow-up method, in which the college first contacts former students to identify their employers and then surveys the employers. Organize survey questions into categories such as field of training, job classification, and specific performance attributes (e.g., specific job skills, work attitude and sense of responsibility, and potential for achievement). Assess multiple attributes of performance and use a Likert-type rating scale of at least five points. We recommend electronic transmission and return of the survey to fit employers' busy schedules. If resources are available, in-depth interviews with employers are also recommended.

CORE INDICATOR 13:
CLIENT SATISFACTION WITH PROGRAMS AND SERVICES

STATISTIC OF INTEREST

The proportion of community college clients who are aware of, have access to, and use the programs and services offered by a college. *Note.* No single statistic currently meets the intent of this indicator.

FREQUENCY OF DATA COLLECTION

At least annually.

RECOMMENDED METHOD

To gather data for this indicator, an institution must determine (a) the array of different clients it serves; (b) the nature, types, and volume of programs and services it provides to different clients; and (c) the extent to which clients are involved in and satisfied with programs and services. Successful reporting of this indicator therefore requires multiple methods of gathering information, such as the following:

- Administer specially designed evaluations to clients participating in programs and services to determine their expectations and the extent to which the experience met, exceeded, or fell short of expectations (e.g., using a Likert scale).
- Conduct periodic surveys with client groups, typically by mail, electronically, or by telephone, using an instrument designed to collect information about clients' involvement and satisfaction with a program or service.
- Gather written reports by professional staff members based on (a) observation of clients participating in programs and services and (b) interviews with clients during and after contact with the program or service.
- Conduct focus group with client groups to determine their involvement in and satisfaction with programs and services.

COMMENTS

The term *client* includes all of the different individuals, groups, and organizations that come into contact with community colleges, including students and employers.

CORE INDICATOR 14:
VALUE ADDED TO THE COMMUNITY

STATISTIC OF INTEREST

The number and types of identified outcomes and benefits received by a community from programs, services, and activities offered by a community college. *Note.* No single statistic satisfies the intent of this indicator. See Comments.

FREQUENCY OF DATA COLLECTION

Ongoing.

RECOMMENDED METHOD

Before undertaking any methodology, colleges should define *value* as a unit of analysis that applies to the specific communities they serve. For a local community, value may be measured in terms of expenditures by a college for personnel, goods, and services that create economic impact; economic development through college-sponsored worker-training programs that attract and retain business and industry; or improvement in the quality of life through rising levels of education and decreasing unemployment and welfare rates. For communities on a regional, state, or national scale, value contributed by a college can be realized in terms of increased competitive capability on a regional, national, or global level and contribution to the economy through enhancement of production and reduction in unemployment and welfare rates. The following are important steps that a college should take to determine the value that it adds to a community, however it is defined:

- On a local scale, identify the boundaries and defining characteristics of the community served by the college (e.g., a county or multicounty region, a city, a suburban area in proximity to a city, etc.).
- On a regional scale, identify (a) the region that is the unit of analysis and (b) the number and types of postsecondary institutions that will be included in the analysis of value added.
- Assess value added through (a) analysis of published statistical data (especially important in analyses of impact at the regional or state level) or (b) analysis of a community's perceptions of a college's contribution through questions in electronic surveys, telephone interviews, and focus groups.

CORE INDICATOR 14 [cont'd]: VALUE ADDED TO THE COMMUNITY

Ask representatives from a cross section of the community to describe the benefits they received in specific areas (e.g., employment opportunities, business and industry attraction and retention, quality of life, etc.).

COMMENTS

Value is a complex concept involving multiple constituencies, multiple levels of analysis, and uniquely held views about what a community college should be doing to meet needs and expectations. The concept of community can be understood in two ways, one distinctly local and the other larger in scale. From a local standpoint, it is "a collectivity of people with common interests living in a particular area." Extended beyond the geography of a locality to a region or state, it is "a body of persons with varied social, economic, or political interests living together in a larger society."

CORE INDICATOR 15: TRANSFER RATES

STATISTIC OF INTEREST

The proportion of an entering student cohort actively enrolled in a degree program at a community college and completing at least 12 semester hours of credit (or the equivalent) who then enroll within two years for at least 12 college-level credits in a degree program at a 4-year college.

FREQUENCY OF DATA COLLECTION

At least annually.

RECOMMENDED METHOD

Obtain actual student record information from transfer institutions, in the following order:

- State-level enrollment information that directly matches students who attend community colleges and 4-year colleges by means of a student identification number.
- Transcript information electronically transferred in a defined format.
- Periodic aggregate reports from 4-year institutions.
- Self-reports obtained from follow-up surveys of former community college students.

ADDITIONAL METHODS

- Report data according to the total number of credits earned at the community college.
- Report data (obtained through a regularly administered survey) according to whether students explicitly indicated an intent to transfer.
- Report the proportion of former community college students enrolling for at least one credit at the transfer institution (thereby relaxing the 12-credit transfer constraint for this indicator).

CORE INDICATOR 16:
PERFORMANCE AFTER TRANSFER

STATISTIC OF INTEREST
The proportion of former community college students completing college-level courses at a transfer institution with a grade of *C* or better, compared to the parallel proportion obtained for students who began their studies at the transfer institution as first-time freshmen.

FREQUENCY OF DATA COLLECTION
At least annually.

RECOMMENDED METHOD
Maintain a continuously updated longitudinal database that tracks the grades of a community college student cohort from entry to exit using elements such as date of initial enrollment, degrees or certificates awarded, and duration of study. Cohorts may be constructed so that they are consistent with (but more inclusive than) those required for current federal and state reporting.

ADDITIONAL METHODS
- Report data according to the number of community college credits earned prior to transfer, in blocks of 15 credits.
- Report data according to whether students earned a degree or certificate before transferring.

CHAPTER 4
Effectiveness Assessment and Accountability

The technical descriptions for the core indicators in the previous chapter provide a foundation for measuring the effectiveness of community colleges in carrying out their missions. By no means, however, do they set a limit on what a college could measure to improve performance. Given conditions of turbulence and change in the external environment, community colleges will want to examine how they function as institutions initiating and responding to change. It will not be enough, for example, to measure student progress and take steps toward enhancement, expecting that a market niche will be created. As we have emphasized throughout this book, an institution's assessment portfolio will need to contain indicators that measure not only what students accomplish, but also the value that they and external stakeholders receive through engagement with programs and services.

The core indicators do not fully address a number of factors that institutions of higher education are being asked to measure in the name of accountability, which are mostly indicators of organizational functioning centered on the efficient use of resources. These indicators often are not attuned to the operational realities of colleges. Nevertheless, community colleges need to focus on finding ways to deal with inappropriate or poorly constructed measures imposed on them by others. Finally, community colleges need to find ways to report information to key stakeholders in a way that will attract attention and support. These venues all have to do with the enhancement of performance using the discipline and methodology of effectiveness assessment.

New Directions for Assessing Institutional Performance

If community colleges are to achieve their full performance potential, they will need to address key aspects of organizational functioning. The following are important dimensions of organizational performance for leaders to consider and monitor, either as contributors to or as proxies for quality.

MULTIPLE AND INNOVATIVE MODES OF DELIVERY

Responding meaningfully to a growing variety of demands by clients requires that community colleges become increasingly flexible in their modes of instruction and service delivery. Providing access to instruction and services anytime and anyplace is a bottom-line expectation of many learners and is now a common practice in community colleges. At the same time, flexible modes of instructional delivery that promise to increase learning are generating more interest and garnering wide support. These include competency-based learning and credentialing systems, collaborative learning, service learning, problem-based models and simulations, and self-paced or asynchronous learning.

These developments require flexibility in administrative structures, systems and processes, and policies guiding instructional and service delivery. Community colleges need to unburden themselves of administrative structures and procedures that slow their ability to implement innovations. Outdated procedures that force course offerings into a term- and credit-based format commonly include the following: time-consuming internal course- and curriculum-approval processes, faculty reward systems, registration procedures, and academic accounting procedures. In addition, colleges need to overcome resistance to innovating instructional delivery because of the amount of work that is involved.

Constructing indicators of a college's capacity to develop and use innovative modes of instruction and service delivery might proceed on several levels. At the most basic level, a college might monitor the proportion of total instructional and service delivery (measured in credit equivalents or enrollment for instruction and the number of student transactions for services) accounted for by nontraditional delivery formats. At a second level, it might examine the rate of change: If change is occurring at a rapid pace, there are probably few organizational barriers to implementation. Following the logic of Core Indicator 9: Responsiveness to Community Needs, a third level might be to examine (1) the average time required to gain internal approval to implement new approaches to instructional and service delivery and (2) the time required to move an innovation from concrete proposal to implementation. Finally, the institution might employ an audit approach and systematically examine the particular organizational barriers, incentives, and disincentives that affect innovative initiatives.

INFORMATION AND RESOURCES FOR PLANNING

Rapidly changing environments place a heavy burden on a college's capacity to plan for the future. However, as many corporations have found, acquiring and acting on a solid base of information is one of the most important ways to ensure vitality in uncertain times. Community colleges need information and planning resources to gain intelligence about trends in the external environment and competitors. This knowledge may, in turn, give the institution an advantage in developing and deploying new programs quickly (and avoiding costly mistakes). Equally important are the information and analytic resources required for an institution to monitor its performance and to undertake continuous improvement. Prominent here are outcomes assessment, measures of stakeholders' satisfaction, and indicators that examine key internal management and support processes. In each of these areas, high performance demands more than just a compendium of data. Information must be widely accessible to staff throughout the institution, and it must be prominently and regularly used in the decision-making process.

Constructing indicators that a college can use to enhance its information and planning resources might also occur at multiple levels. A first step might be to simply examine current levels of institutional investment in these resources—expenditures for administrative computing, data acquisition through external scanning, and institutional research and planning—as a percentage of the total operating budget. A good benchmark might be 2% to 5% of total expenditures, which is the standard commonly applied in industry for research and development.

At the next level, a college can assess the adequacy of available information and analytic resources through its ability to efficiently produce useful analytical statistics from its current data bank. Can the institution readily calculate multifaceted performance indicators such as the percentage of first-time students taught by part-time instructors, the probability of a given first-term learner being enrolled in a class with fewer than 20 students, or the performance of students in their first course requiring proficiency subsequent to completing a developmental course? A third level might document how easily a given member of the college community might obtain such data.

Finally, an audit approach might best determine the actual use of information in decision making. Here, a particular decision might be examined systematically to determine the kinds of information made available and considered, or regular internal communications (memos, newsletters, meeting minutes) might be scanned to determine the inclusion of or references to relevant data.

ASSET MAINTENANCE AND DEVELOPMENT

A critical component of effectiveness is the ability of an institution to accomplish valued purposes related to both its mission and its stakeholders through the appropriate use of resources. A purely outcomes-driven definition of effectiveness can obscure the fact that high rates of so-called production, in the short run, might be attained by reducing investment in key assets. Indeed, this is often what happens in periods of funding shortfall: Roofs do not get repaired, equipment does not get replaced, and faculty- and staff-development efforts may be scaled back or cease altogether. Allowing such assets to depreciate is rarely good practice in the long run and will ultimately diminish a college's performance on important outcome measures. Renewing key assets on a regular basis effectively positions an institution to accommodate important changes in technology and to quickly adopt new instructional or administrative practices that may result in significant long-term improvements in effectiveness.

Constructing indicators that address effective stewardship of key assets is usually straightforward. Most such measures are defined as ratios between the current value of an asset and the amount that the institution spends annually to maintain or to renew it. Examples include the following:

- The ratio of annual expenditures on facilities repair and renewal versus the current replacement value of the physical plant (usually benchmarked at about 2%).
- The ratio of annual expenditures on equipment versus the local book value on current equipment (usually benchmarked at 10% to 15%).
- The ratio of annual expenditures on faculty and staff development versus total personnel compensation. Or the percentage of the total course inventory in a given program represented by newly developed or redesigned courses (a measure of curriculum renewal).

Measures like these are never adequate in and of themselves to demonstrate institutional effectiveness. They are important, however, because they involve organizational factors that are inextricably linked to high performance.

Externally Imposed Measures

Direct measures of efficiency tend to dominate the thinking of policymakers and resource providers and reflect their desire to shape or control institutional behavior. It is important to stress to those with an influence over resource provision that effectiveness is about outcomes, not processes. Effective organizations distribute operational management responsibilities to the lowest feasible level and hold unit managers largely responsible for outcomes. As long as managers achieve desired results on time and within cost, they should be given the freedom to deploy institutional resources as they see fit. Policymakers and resource providers should be reminded that directly mandating institutional behavior is not likely to result in high performance. This argument is not likely to prevail in difficult political circumstances; therefore, it is important to be aware of the pitfalls implicit in some of the most common measures by which external constituencies judge institutional effectiveness.

FACULTY WORKLOAD

Direct measures of faculty workload are now common for many public colleges and universities. This trend reflects a number of external concerns. One that is applicable to 4-year colleges is the contention that faculty should spend more time on teaching. Underlying this sentiment is a general public perception that faculty do not spend much time on any one part of their job. Demands for greater efficiency will always center on faculty, if only because faculty time is the dominant resource at all institutions.

Measuring faculty workload is a tricky business. A primary concern is what to count as work. The most common workload measures are based on ratios between the number of faculty and teaching outputs such as number of students taught or credit hours generated. These ratios are pure productivity measures, however, and may or may not reflect the real effort involved. An instructor who teaches a class with 50 students may seem twice as productive as one who teaches a class of 25, but is that instructor really working twice as hard? Both instructors must design and deliver the same number of class sessions, although from a productivity standpoint, they have different numbers of assignments to grade.

A second approach involves the number of courses or sections taught—an approach that ignores many critical functions that instructors provide, such as advising students, designing new courses and curricula, or engaging in public service. A third approach tries to measure time allocations directly through surveys of faculty activity. Such surveys are notoriously unreliable because people may differ in how they report particular kinds of tasks. When faced with these three alternatives and forced to make a decision, community colleges are probably best advised to adopt the first approach. But in doing so, leaders should indicate clearly that the resulting statistic can be interpreted only as an overall institutional efficiency measure, not as a measure of how much work faculty actually do.

Two additional issues are likely to affect discussions of workload: part-time instructors and the use of technology. Concerns about quality often prompt mandates to measure the proportion of instruction provided by part-time faculty. This measure may be inappropriate for a community college, because the use of part-time professionals, who are as well if not better prepared than their full-time counterparts, is critical for many career and technical programs. Technology also muddies the water with respect to workload by inflating the number of students faculty can reach using distance-learning technology. In distance-delivery courses, for example, a single instructor may reach hundreds of students with the same lecture. At the same time, other instructors may be "coaching" students individually through computer-based skill development modules in which students move at their own pace and do not generate traditional credits. Learning situations of this type are becoming increasingly common and promise to increase substantially in the years ahead. Capturing them fully as part of a faculty workload measure is practically impossible.

INSTRUCTIONAL COSTS

As emphasized earlier, attention to principles and practices of cost-effectiveness is an important component of overall effectiveness. This implies that community colleges should examine instructional costs as part of their internal management systems. Using cost statistics alone as a direct measure of effectiveness for external accountability purposes, however, raises numerous issues.

Because instruction is the single largest "factor of production" in community college operations, most instructional cost measures are really variants of faculty productivity measures. Outcomes are typically counted in the form of credits generated or students taught. Costs, in turn, are counted in terms of the salary dollars allocated to the instructor teaching each course. The principal difficulty here is that instructors' salaries vary considerably based on factors that have nothing to do with productivity, especially seniority and market factors associated with hiring and retraining instructors in particular academic and professional fields. Colleges with a unique disciplinary mix—for example, one focused on health care and technology training—may bear naturally higher costs than those providing instruction in an array of different fields.

The approach of using cost statistics also ignores the increasing importance of technology and instructional equipment in community college teaching. Directly accounting for all costs in relationship to instructional outputs can be a formidable task and will most likely amplify the effects of differences in disciplinary mix. Indeed, one of the most pernicious effects of pure efficiency measures is that they may induce institutions to restrict instructional offerings in high-demand fields (e.g., engineering technology and health care) that involve substantial equipment and technology outlays.

NUMBER OF DEGREES GRANTED

The total number of degrees granted by an institution has also been frequently advanced as a measure of community college effectiveness. The rationale used for degree completion is the same as that prompting the use of persistence and retention statistics: Community colleges do not produce sufficient numbers of program completers given the number of students they enroll. The misleading assumption here is that degree production is the only business that community colleges should be in. Although program completion may be important for some students who enroll, it will not be a goal of many others.

Community colleges could address this problem by surveying incoming students to determine their actual goals. Colleges should ensure that information related to degree granting is always accompanied by information describing students'goals at entry and beyond. A second way to address the problem is to emphasize statistics related to the completion of other goals. With the continuing development of competency-based instructional options, certification of achievement or mastery may become increasingly common. Reporting the number and proportion of students completing intermediate goals in education—that is, more than a course but less than a degree—may also help mitigate the negative implications for community colleges of pure degree-production statistics.

TIME TO DEGREE AND EXCESS COURSE TAKING

Another accountability issue for all colleges is the time it takes students to attain a degree. Most often this takes the form of a focus on the number of students taking what appear to be more courses than necessary to complete a program, thereby limiting access for others. Community colleges should resist time-to-degree measures. We know that substantial numbers of students enrolled in community colleges complete degrees many years after they first enroll. This is usually because pressures associated with work, family, and community require them to attend part time or to interrupt enrollment. Providing education at times and places that are convenient for learners is what community colleges are about, particularly in a job market in which lifelong learning is essential. Imposing a linear model on community colleges, in which full-time students moving steadily toward degrees is the norm, serves to encourage colleges to ignore the needs of students who have different life circumstances. Part-time attendance and discontinuous patterns of enrollment are largely outside an institution's control. They also are a burgeoning reality for all colleges as students move into, out of, and between institutions in pursuit of convenience.

Excess-credit measures pose a similar problem because course taking, again, is largely a matter of choice. Degree completion is rarely the only objective of a student who enrolls in a community college. Many decide on a degree only after completing a number of courses. Others will take courses because of specific interests or job-related needs, even though the courses are not required for program completion. Finally, available statistics do not suggest that excess course taking is a particular problem for community colleges. For the most commonly used measure, the ratio of total credits actually completed by program graduates versus the number required for program completion (usually called a "graduation efficiency index"), community colleges generally achieve greater than 90% efficiency. Statistics on excess course taking should not unduly concern most colleges.

Responding to Externally Imposed Measures

Policymakers are becoming increasingly active in imposing linear measures of organizational performance on community colleges, in large part because of concerns about cost and accountability. As a result, virtually all community colleges will encounter occasions when such measures are advocated. The following suggestions may be helpful to a community college faced with this circumstance.

LEAD WITH CORE INDICATORS

We constructed the core indicators around a model of institutional effectiveness that is appropriate for community colleges and is supported by experience. Based primarily on outcomes, the core indicators focus on what stakeholders want from the institutions they invest in. Actively leading accountability-related discussions by emphasizing outcome-related core indicators demonstrates that an institution is willing to be held accountable. At the same time, it helps direct attention away from areas of institutional functioning that should be a matter of internal management discretion.

EMPHASIZE OTHER KEY OUTCOMES

If outcomes are the real bottom line of institutional effectiveness, only those areas of organizational functioning that are demonstrably related to outcomes should be considered. If external constituents insist on measuring organizational functioning, college leaders should remind them that concepts such as organizational flexibility and responsiveness, information resources, quality assurance processes, and the stewardship of key assets are the more appropriate areas to consider. More importantly, community colleges should be able to demonstrate that they are already looking into these matters internally and making continuous improvements based on what they find.

DEFINE MEANINGFUL MEASURES

Actively participate in the process of identifying and defining measures that reflect the realities of community college clientele and operations. At a time of growing interest in accountability, externally mandated involvement in some kind of performance-indicator system is almost unavoidable. When performance measures are proposed, the appropriate response should be to actively work with authorities to make the resulting measures as meaningful as they can possibly be. Active resistance to measurement from the outset will only increase pressure in return and will most likely result in the eventual imposition of poorly constructed measures.

Even the most narrow and inappropriate of measures usually can be modified to take into account the particular environment in which community colleges operate and the clientele they serve. Often those who advocate inappropriate indicators do not understand the service market in which community colleges work and how different it is from that of 4-year colleges. Faced with persuasive arguments, authorities may be willing to consider and accept alternatives that meet the basic intent of accountability.

SUPPORT ALL STATISTICS

Statistical indicators, no matter how well constructed, are always open to misuse and misinterpretation. As a result, college leaders are well advised to report problematic statistics together with additional information that helps explain why the numbers look the way they do. Often this information will consist of facts demonstrating that the college has achieved higher levels of performance. For example, supplement 3-year program-completion rates as mandated by HEA disclosure requirements with program-completion rates at 4, 5, 6, or more years. This information may consist of additional breakdowns of the reported statistics. An institution may want to show that its instruction costs appear high in terms of total dollars per credit hour because it offers an unusually high proportion of technology-intensive programs that its constituents want and need. In other cases, the accompanying information may consist of important contextual descriptors of the population served—emphasizing, for instance, that the college's student body includes a high proportion of first-generation or underprepared students or students whose primary objective is not to seek a degree. Almost always, the information that a community college supplies should be accompanied by statements that describe implications for action, together with what the institution plans to do (or is already doing) to address these implications.

External demands for information are unpredictable and sometimes unreasonable, but they are likely to increase markedly in the years ahead. By taking a proactive stance in responding to such demands, acknowledging their legitimacy and helping to move the discussion in a more appropriate direction, community colleges can demonstrate their effectiveness and avoid, at least in part, being unfairly judged.

APPROACHES TO REPORTING

The reporting and use of effectiveness data has been a continuing challenge for leaders and institutions alike. When effectiveness first appeared on the radar screens of community colleges in the mid-1980s, the challenge was one of figuring out what to measure and why as part of an effort to get assessment systems up and running. In the larger and more complex institutions that colleges have become today, the challenge is one of getting maximum value out of effectiveness information. Leaders know that information is of little value unless it can be used in some way to improve performance. They also know that to be effectively used, information must be easy to read and understand—it must be organized and reported well.

There are a number of different approaches that colleges can use to report information, each with its advantages and disadvantages. In the following sections are descriptions of five of the more promising approaches. Constituency-based reporting and the community scorecard are aimed at external stakeholders as beneficiaries of institutional programs and services. Mission-based, challenge, and functional-area reporting are keyed to internal stakeholders and performance at the individual, unit, and institutional levels and are related to mission, operations, and challenges affecting institutional development.

CONSTITUENCY-BASED REPORTING

A key principle involved in building and maintaining relationships with external stakeholders is the meaningful disclosure of performance information. One way to provide this information is to prepare an Institutional Performance Statement (see Table 5.1) customized to different stakeholder groups external to the institution. This statement

- Identifies the stakeholder group that is, or will be, the recipient of effectiveness information
- Explains the relationship of the group to the institution by describing the value it seeks in terms of performance expectations
- Articulates and defines indicators that will be used to measure and report performance
- Reports data describing performance outcomes generated for each indicator by the institution

Could a disclosure of this type to external stakeholders involve risks and costs that would offset any gain to the institution? The reality is that stakeholders who are associated with well-managed profit and nonprofit organizations are accustomed to the type of information contained in an institutional performance statement. Indeed, the absence of such information could provide more incentive for questioning leaders about institutional performance than could its availability. In an environment that encourages community colleges to strive for a "culture of evidence," performance-driven institutions have a real opportunity to achieve gains with stakeholders simply by reporting effectiveness information that is clear and compelling (see Alfred, 2003).

Table 5.1 Institutional Performance Statement	
Employers' (Stakeholders') Performance Expectations	**Core Indicator**
Workers trained in community colleges will have well-developed general education competencies and technical skills that enable them to perform at a satisfactory or better level on the job.	Employer Satisfaction With Graduates Placement Rates
Workers will be capable of stepping into a new job and performing required tasks without a need for retraining.	Clients Satisfaction With Programs and Services
Workers will possess soft skills that enable them to learn on the job, work collaboratively with peers, and communicate effectively with customers.	Demonstration of General Education Competencies
Data Outlay and Analysis _____ _____ _____ _____ _____	

COMMUNITY SCORECARD

Effectiveness reporting that is focused on creating a scorecard for the community typically identifies goals that a college has created for serving a community (or important constituencies within a community) and delineates measures and targets for performance that relate to these goals. The college then tabulates results for each measure at specified intervals and reports them to the community. For example, a community college might build its scorecard around three key dimensions of its relationship with the community—engagement in education, value added, and community development—using the following measures of performance:

- Participation rate—the proportion of the population aged 17 and older that has participated in an organized activity sponsored by the college in the past year.

- College-going rate—the percentage of students graduating from high school entering the college within one year of graduation.
- Workforce development—the proportion of business and industry employees enrolled in college courses during the past year.
- Placement rate in workforce—the proportion of an entering student cohort achieving a marketable skill and obtaining employment in a field directly related to that skill.
- Business and industry attraction and retention—the number of businesses citing a community college as a reason for attraction to, or retention in, a community.
- Response to community needs—the number of programs and services created and delivered to the community by a college in the past year.

A sample scorecard format is depicted in Table 5.2. Note that the scorecard should not be just a collection of measures simply considered to be important to the community. A well-developed scorecard will reflect needs and expectations of the community determined through assessment carried out with representative groups. A good test of a scorecard's efficacy is the ability to determine the value the community seeks from a college by looking at the scorecard in isolation from supporting data and information.

MISSION-BASED REPORTING
Mission-based reporting is organized and carried out in the same way as performance-based reporting with the exception that performance measures are

Table 5.2 Community Scorecard			
Performance Measure	2004–2005	2005–2006	% Improvement
Participation Rate			
College-Going Rate			
Workforce Development			
Placement Rate in Workforce			
Business/Attraction Retention			
Response to Community Needs			

aligned with components of the institution's mission. A mission (transfer preparation, student progress, workforce development, etc.) is identified; institutional goals for performance are specified; indicators for measuring goal achievement are delineated; and data are gathered, analyzed, and reported. A simple example will show how mission-based reporting works.

An important mission for most community colleges is transfer preparation. Assume that your college is actively engaged in preparing students for transfer and has established two goals for performance in this arena: (1) a minimum of 30% of an entering student cohort will transfer to a 4-year institution within 4 years after initial enrollment, and (2) the majority of students who transfer will perform as well as or better than their 4-year counterparts in the last 2 years of college. The indicators that will be used to measure performance are transfer rates and performance after transfer.

Data related to these indicators will be gathered and analyzed and a summary report prepared and released to constituencies requiring documentation of institutional performance. Consider formatting the report as an Institutional Performance Statement (see page 54), presenting missions, performance goals, and performance indicators in alignment with one another and presenting performance data and analysis in a summary statement for each mission.

CHALLENGE REPORTING

Similar to the community scorecard, the objective of challenge reporting is to measure and report performance in relationship to specific challenges facing the institution or priorities it has identified for resource allocation. Community colleges routinely develop priorities as a product of strategic planning or through assessment efforts related to accreditation, bond campaigns, and private sector fundraising. Challenge reporting differs from the scorecard, however, in that it uses a specific set of indicators that describe institutional performance in relationship to a particular challenge or priority. For example, High-Performing Community College has identified student retention as a major challenge it must address and as a priority for resource allocation in the next budget year. It has determined that 12 indicators are important for measuring its performance in retention, which are depicted in Table 5.3.

Report performance by organizing these indicators into a flow model and charting data for each indicator annually. As longitudinal performance data

Table 5.3 Indicators of Student Retention		
ENTRY	**THROUGHPUT**	**EXIT**
1. Students' goals at entry	4. Hours working per week	11. Quality of service by staff
2. Enrollment status (full-time/part-time)	5. Pattern of enrollment (linear/nonlinear)	12. Clarity of process for re-admission
3. Date of high school graduation/ last college attendance	6. Course taking pattern (synchronous/asynchronous)	
	7. Change of goal	
	8. College GPA	
	9. Use of support services	
	10. Satisfaction with courses/ services	

become available, run year-to-year comparisons for the indicators individually and in combination to create a composite index of performance. For most institutions, challenge reporting will not be limited to one area of performance, but will be carried out for three or four areas that pose developmental challenges for the college. Depending on the gravity of an institution's circumstances, it may be possible or desirable to organize the entire effectiveness program around challenge reporting.

FUNCTIONAL-AREA REPORTING
Although effectiveness assessment is best carried out as a collegewide responsibility, invariably some indicators will become the responsibility of specific units depending on the roles and functions they perform within the college. Clearly the design and management of databases related to effectiveness indicators is beyond the ability of any one unit to coordinate. It is important, therefore, to understand relationships among units in managing and reporting effectiveness data.

The model for functional area reporting of effectiveness information (see Figure 5.1) calls for different functional areas (academic affairs, business services, student development, etc.) to take responsibility for the management of core indicators—that is, for gathering and formatting data and disclosing findings. Methods for data collection and formatting are agreed upon in advance, and each unit works independently to piece together data for specific indicators. Although a data-management and reporting arrangement of this type is

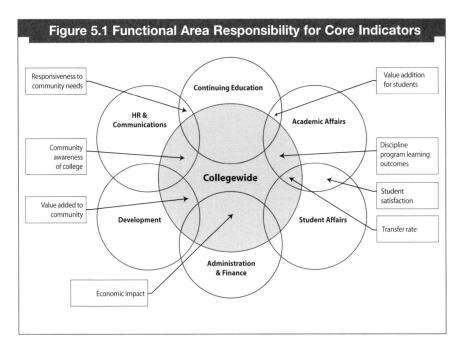

Figure 5.1 Functional Area Responsibility for Core Indicators

Responsiveness to community needs

Value addition for students

Continuing Education

HR & Communications

Academic Affairs

Community awareness of college

Discipline program learning outcomes

Collegewide

Student satisfaction

Value added to community

Development

Student Affairs

Transfer rate

Administration & Finance

Economic impact

certainly not ideal, it is a reality for many institutions that lack resources to maintain an independent office or assessment function.

＞―◆＞―○―◇―◇―＜

These reporting methods are but five that can be used to report effectiveness results. They are not intended to be prescriptive or adopted for use in their current form. Rather, they provide a framework for integrating thought and action in effectiveness by linking the *why* and *who* underlying effectiveness (Why are we assessing effectiveness? and Who will be receiving and interpreting the results?) with the *what* and *how* associated with measuring effectiveness and reporting results (What indicators can be used to measure performance? and How do we operationalize them and report the results?). Regardless of the reporting method used, the analysis and discussion of effectiveness results should yield an accurate and balanced description of the outcomes of a college's programs and services rather than be used to justify a college's current performance.

CHAPTER 5

Tomorrow's Playing Field

The year is 2012 and the institution is Niche Community College, a single-campus institution located in a suburban community with a lucrative tax base. Since its establishment in 1964, Niche has maintained a steady course in pursuit of its mission of preparing students for transfer, responding to business and industry needs, and providing programs and services to the community. It is highly visible and has received continuing support from the community in recognition of its role as a conduit to better jobs and enhanced income through accessible programs and services. Niche has been unchallenged as an educational force in the region until recently, when the competitive landscape began to change.

In the past year, a for-profit college owned and subsidized by a multinational corporation started offering degrees and programs in direct competition with Niche. It quickly established relationships with local businesses, was nimble and flexible in its program and service offerings, and used savvy marketing techniques to reach working adults. At the same time, a regional teaching university began offering associate degrees through its branch campus and guaranteed full credit toward the bachelor's degree for all work completed at the branch campus.

In and of themselves, these competitive challenges would be sufficient to cut into the market share of most colleges, but competition was not the only problem facing Niche. Inflated oil prices and the exportation of managerial and technological jobs beginning in 2006 prompted high school students and adult learners to consider their college options more carefully. The combination of increased costs for transportation and diminished job prospects led to an enrollment decline that adversely affected revenue as state appropriations were scaled back to correspond with enrollment.

Facing a cutback in state aid, Niche moved to plug the budget gap by announcing an increase in tuition and fees to take effect over the three-year period 2008–2012. The increase elevated the cost of attendance to 70% of the cost of attending the branch campus of the regional university. The impact of this move was catastrophic. Niche had been operating for years on a strategy of lower cost while competitors were operating on a strategy of increased value. With out-of-pocket costs similar to those at a neighboring institution, Niche lost students to a competitor who was delivering the same or better value to stakeholders at a comparable cost. To regain the advantage it once enjoyed, Niche would need to find new and better ways to deliver value. This is where effectiveness comes in.

The first lesson implicit in the experience of Niche Community College is that in the future, effectiveness will be all about value. The benefits created by an institution for its stakeholders and how they stack up against those created by competitors will become the most critical determinant of effectiveness. Colleges will not realize effectiveness in a static or absolute sense, but more as a matter of relativity implicit in a dynamic tension between institutions as they jockey for competitive position.

The second lesson is that, in a tangible sense, effectiveness will include growth in numbers (i.e., graduation, transfer, regional market penetration, or placement rates), evidence of stakeholders' satisfaction, enhancement in quality, and improvement in tangible assets of just about any kind (see Alfred, 2005). We live in a world, however, in which intangible assets are becoming ever more important. Organizational theorists and policymakers point to the growing importance of intangibles as a key part of the playing field on which institutions will compete. Intangibles such as ideas, competencies, quality, and image have a lot to do with success and are so closely intertwined with value that it is almost impossible to separate them from aspects that are tangible. Hence, community colleges will need to take both tangible and intangible determinants of value into account in efforts to assess effectiveness.

The third and final lesson conveyed by the Niche example is that community colleges will need to do much more in the future to learn what is valued by their stakeholders. In our experience, colleges seldom penetrate the minds of stakeholders to uncover their innermost needs, hopes, and expectations. They almost always start with *what is* in terms of easily documented outcomes (e.g., student satisfaction) in contrast to *what could be* in the minds of stakeholders (see Alfred, 2005). An incremental approach to effectiveness assessment that is focused on easily measured outcomes in a world of profound change is unlikely to uncover new or hidden forms of value. This approach works well when the ingredients of value are stable and predictable. But in postsecondary education, as in all industries, these ingredients are no longer stable. They are being altered not only by new competitors, but also by seismic shifts in the economy, technology, demographics, the regulatory environment, and the world order. An incremental approach to effectiveness assessment is well suited to the challenge of extending existing forms of value. However, it is not suited to the challenge of creating new forms of value.

>—+—♦—O—♦—+—<

These lessons capture our view of tomorrow's playing field for effectiveness. Our point of view emphasizes an expanded arena for institutional effectiveness assessment comprising demanding stakeholders and unbridled competitors, a keen appreciation of the role that value will play in effectiveness, and a sensitivity to the growing importance of intangible assets as factors in effectiveness. Implicit in all of this is an urgency for community colleges to transform the results of assessment into actions that enhance programs and services, to provide more value to learners, and to share assessment results with stakeholders.

REFERENCES

Alfred, R. (1998). From closed to open systems: New designs for effectiveness in community colleges. *Community College Journal, 5*(1), 9–19.

Alfred, R. (2000). Assessment as a strategic weapon. *Community College Journal, 70*(4), 12–18.

Alfred, R. (2003). Designing research for organizational change: From analysis to advantage. *Journal of Applied Research in the Community College, 10*(1), 77–87.

Alfred, R. (2005). *Managing the big picture in colleges and universities: From tactics to strategy.* Westport, CT: ACE/Praeger and Greenwood Press.

Alfred, R., & Kreider, P. (1991). Creating a culture for institutional effectiveness. *Community College Journal, 61*(5), 34–40.

Ewell, P. T. (1992). Outcomes assessment, institutional effectiveness, and accreditation. In *Accreditation, assessment and institutional effectiveness: Resource papers for the COPA task force on institutional effectiveness.* Washington, DC: Council on Postsecondary Accreditation. (ERIC No. ED343513)

Ewell, P., Parker, R., & Jones, D. (1988). *Establishing a longitudinal student tracking system: An implementation handbook.* Boulder, CO: National Center for Higher Education Management Systems.

Levine, A., & Cureton, J.S. (1998). Callegiate Life: An Obituary. Change, 30 (3), 12–17, 51.

McClenney, K. (1998). Community colleges perched at the millennium: Perspectives on innovation, transformation, and tomorrow. *Leadership Abstracts, 11*(9).

National Center for Public Policy in Higher Education. (2006). *Measuring up 2006: The national report card on higher education.* Sacramento, CA: Author.

Palmer, J. (1990). *Accountability through student tracking.* Washington, DC: American Association of Community Colleges.

INDEX

Note. Italic type indicates figures, and bold type indicates tables.

technical description, 38

community, value added to. *See* value added to the community (core indicator 14)

community as concept, 40

community needs, responsiveness to. *See* responsiveness to community needs (core indicator 9)

community relations. *See* contribution to the public good mission; outreach mission

community scorecards, 53, 54–**55**

competitiveness issues. *See* globalization

competitors, new, 2–3, 59–60

compulsory indicators category, 19, *22*

computer technology. *See* technology

constituency-based reporting, 53, **54**

context for effectiveness
advanced technology, 4–5
changing markets, 1–3
emergence of networks, 7
globalization, vi–vii, 3–4
implications of effectiveness, 8
new competitors, 2–3
performance and accountability, 5–7

contribution to the public good mission
model differences, vii
modeling core indicators, 16–17
technical description of core indicators, **23,** 39–40

core indicators, defined, 12

See also technical descriptions of core indicators; *specific indicators and aspects*

corporate training programs, 3

cost considerations. *See* financial considerations

course-embedded assessment, 30

course syllabi, 31

courses taught approach to workload measures, 47–48

cross-sectional surveys, 37

curriculum guides, 31

Dd

data reporting and use
approaches to, 52–58
information and resources for planning, 45–46
stage model for assessment, 18–20
See also technical descriptions of core indicators; *specific aspects*

database use, 25, 42, 57

decentralization, and networks, 7

defining and measuring core indicators, 11–12

degrees granted, measuring efficiency, 49

demography
and outreach mission, 15
responsiveness to community needs indicator, 34
and technology impact, 5

demonstration of general education competencies (core indicator 7)
mission relationship to, 15

technical description, 30–31
distance delivery
    context for effectiveness, 3, 5
    faculty workload measures, 48

Ee

efficiency
    assessing effectiveness, 10–13
    externally imposed measures,
        47–52
electronic surveys
    client satisfaction with programs
        and services indicator, 38
    employer satisfaction with
        graduates indicator, 37
    licensure and certification pass
        rates indicator, 36
    placement rates indicator, 35
    responsiveness to community
        needs indicator, 33
    student satisfaction indicator, 27
    value added to the community
        indicator, 39
embedded assessment, 30
employer satisfaction with gradu-
    ates (core indicator 12)
    stage model for assessment, 19
    technical description, 37
employment information, state, 35
engagement indicators category,
    19–20, *22*
environmental scanning processes,
    33–34
Europe, globalization effects, 3
examinations
    embedded assessment, 30
    licensing, 29
excess course taking, measuring

efficiency, 50
externally imposed measures of effi-
    ciency, 47–52

Ff

faculty workload, measuring effi-
    ciency, 47–48
financial considerations
    accountability and effectiveness
        assessment, 45, 46, 50
    assessing effectiveness, 9–11
    institutional performance
        statement, 53
    instructional cost measurement,
        48–49
    Niche Community College
        example, 59–61
    stage model for assessment,
        18–20
    support of statistics, 52
flow model, in challenge reporting,
    56
focus groups, 33, 38, 39
for-profit higher education compa-
    nies
    changing markets, 2
    performance and accountability,
        6
functional-area reporting, 53, 57–*58*
future playing field for effectiveness,
    vii–viii, 59–61

Gg

general education competencies.
    See demonstration of general
        education competencies
        (core indicator 7)

general education mission
model differences, vii
modeling core indicators, 14–15
technical description of core indicators, **23,** 28–31
globalization
accountability and competitiveness, 6
context for effectiveness, vi–vii, 3–4
mission relationship to core indicators, 16, 17
grades, technical descriptions of core indicators, 28, 42
graduation efficiency index, described, 50
graduation rates, reporting of, 5
graduation rates (core indicator 3)
mission relationship to, 14–15
modeling core indicators, 14
technical description, 26

Hh

headcounts and attendance figures, 32
High-Performing Community College example, 56, **57**
Higher Education Act (HEA), 5, 25, 26, 52
holistic scoring rubrics, 30

Ii

in-class surveys, 27
in-depth interviews, 37
India, globalization effects, 3
indicators, defined, 11, 12

innovating instruction and service delivery, 44–45
institutional capacity, 5, 6, 13
See also resource constraints
institutional performance statement, 53, **54,** 56
instruction and service delivery, innovation in, 44–45
instructional costs, measuring efficiency, 48–49
instructor workload, measuring efficiency, 47–48
intangibles, growing importance of, 60
internal audits, 34

Ji

job placement information, 35

Kk

key elements of effectiveness, *10*
key outcomes, emphasizing, 51

Ll

licensing examinations, 29
licensure and certification pass rates (core indicator 11)
mission relationship to, 16
technical description, 36
Likert scale use, 24, 27, 37, 38

Mm

macro impact indicators category, 19–20, *22*
mail surveys, 27, 35, 36, 38

market changes
    context for effectiveness, 1–3
    and workforce development
        mission, 16
meaningful measures, defining, 51
measurement guidelines, checklist
    for, 12
mission
    and accountability, 6
    defining core indicators, 12
    defining effectiveness, 9–11, 13
    mission-based reporting, 53,
        55–56
    model differences, vii
    modeling core indicators,
        13, 21
    Niche Community College
        example, 59
    relationship to core indicators,
        13–18
    technical description of core
        indicators, **23**
    See also specific missions
modeling core indicators,
    13, 21
modes of instruction and service
    delivery, innovation in, 44–45
Motorola, 3

Nn

National Center for Public Policy
    and Higher Education, 6
networks, emergence of, 7
    See also partnerships
Niche Community College exam-
    ple, 59–61

Oo

offshoring and outsourcing. *See*
    globalization
open-ended survey design, 37
outcomes, defined, 11
outreach mission
    modeling core indicators,
        15–16
    technical description of core
        indicators, **23,** 32–34

Pp

part-time instructors, faculty work-
    load measures, 48
part-time students
    graduation rates core indicator,
        26
    time-to-degree measures, 50
partnerships
    context for effectiveness, 2, 5, 7
    responsiveness to community
        needs indicator, 34
performance after transfer (core
    indicator 16)
    mission relationship to, 17
    technical description, 42
performance and accountability,
    5–7
performance statement, institution-
    al, 53, **54,** 56
persistence (core indicator 2)
    mission relationship to, 14–15
    reporting recommendation, 26
    technical description, 25
placement rates (core indicator 10)
    technical description, 35
planning

state licensing agencies, 36

statistics, support of, 52

student goal attainment (core indicator 1)

mission relationship to, 14

stage model for assessment, 19

technical description, 24

student needs and expectations, changes in, 1–2

See also stakeholder needs and expectations

student portfolios, 30

student progress mission

defining core indicators, 12

modeling core indicators, 13

relationship to core indicators, 14

technical description of core indicators, **23,** 24–27

student record information, 41

student retention, indicators of, 56, **57**

Student Right-to-Know and Campus Security Act, 5

student satisfaction (core indicator 4)

mission relationship to, 14

stage model for assessment, 19

technical description, 27

students lacking in basic skills, 28

success in subsequent and related course work (core indicator 5)

mission relationship to, 15

technical description, 28

survey methodology. *See* technical descriptions of core indicators

Tt

technical descriptions of core indicators, **23**

1. student goal attainment, 24
2. persistence, 25
3. graduation rates, 26
4. student satisfaction, 27
5. success in subsequent and related course work, 28
6. program learning outcomes and mastery of discipline, 29
7. demonstration of general education competencies, 30–31
8. regional market penetration rates, 32
9. responsiveness to community needs, 33–34
10. placement rates, 35
11. licensure and certification pass rates, 36
12. employer satisfaction with graduates, 37
13. client satisfaction with programs and services, 38
14. value added to the community, 39–40
15. transfer rates, 41
16. performance after transfer, 42

See also specific indicators and aspects

technology

context for effectiveness, 4–5

measures of efficiency, 48, 49

workforce development mission, 16

telephone surveys, 33, 35, 38, 39

testing, standardized, 30

time allocations approach to workload measures, 48
time to attain degree, measuring
efficiency, 49–50
transfer preparation mission
mission-based reporting, 56
modeling core indicators,
17–18
technical description of core
indicators, **23,** 41–42
transfer rates (core indicator 15)
mission relationship to, 17
technical description, 41

Uu

United States
competitiveness issues, 6, 17
Internet use data, 4
University of Phoenix, 2, 3
U.S. Department of Education, 5
use and reporting of data. *See* data
reporting and use

Vv

value added to the community
(core indicator 14)
mission relationship to, 17
stage model for assessment, 20
technical description, 39–40
value as concept, 39, 40

Ww

workforce development mission
modeling core indicators,
16
technical description of core
indicators, **23,** 35–38
workload of faculty, measuring
efficiency, 47–48

ABOUT THE AUTHORS

Richard Alfred is professor of higher education at the University of Michigan and founding director of the Center for Community College Development. During a 38-year career in higher education, he has held executive-level positions in community colleges in Cleveland, Kansas City, and New York City; created and served as a principal in the Center for Community College Development; and developed organizational strategy, strategic plans, and effectiveness models for 200 colleges in the United States and Canada. Alfred is the author of more than 100 books, articles, and monographs on the topic of leadership and management in colleges and universities. His most recent book, *Managing the Big Picture in Colleges and Universities: From Tactics to Strategy* (ACE/Praeger, 2005), was the 2006 winner of the Alice Beeman Award for Published Scholarship presented by the Council for Advancement and Support of Education. A recipient of numerous honors and awards including the AACC Leadership Award, his highest priority is campus-based work with community colleges in designing and managing organizational change. Alfred holds master's and doctoral degrees in higher education and sociology from Penn State University and a bachelor's degree from Allegheny College.

Christopher Shults holds a master's degree from the University of Michigan and is a doctoral candidate in organizational behavior and management in the Center for the Study of Higher and Postsecondary Education at the University of Michigan. Prior to entering doctoral study, he served as research associate at AACC, where he wrote research briefs. While at Michigan, he has written on topics of institutional effectiveness and organizational strategy, created an innovative leadership development program for minority-serving institutions, developed courses on leadership, and lectured on the topic of strategy in several universities.

Jeffrey Seybert is director of institutional research, evaluation, and instructional development at Johnson County Community College in Overland Park,

Kansas. Prior to his appointment at Johnson County, he served as assistant professor of psychology at the University of Missouri-Kansas City. Seybert is past president of the National Community College Council for Research and Planning and the Mid-America Association for Institutional Research and has served on the board of directors of the Association for Institutional Research. He serves as a consulting editor for the *Journal of Applied Research in the Community College* and the *AIR Professional File* and as consulting editor and contributing columnist for *Assessment Update*. He has published more than 50 articles and book chapters and has served as a consultant to more than 100 nonprofit and for-profit organizations. Seybert holds a baccalaureate in psychology from California State University-Long Beach, and a master's degree (public administration) and doctoral degree (experimental psychology) from the University of Missouri-Kansas City.